Existentialism and Humanism

Jean-Paul Sartre

philosophy
in focus

Gerald Jones
Daniel Cardinal
Jeremy Hayward

Academic consultant
Nigel Warburton

JOHN MURRAY

Authors

Gerald Jones is Head of Humanities at the Mary Ward Centre, London; **Daniel Cardinal** is Head of Philosophy at Orpington College and teaches Philosophy at Birkbeck Faculty of Continuing Education; **Jeremy Hayward** is a lecturer at the Institute of Education, London, where he is the subject leader for the PGCE in Citizenship education.

The academic consultant **Nigel Warburton** is a Senior Lecturer at the Open University. He is also the author of *Philosophy: The Basics* (currently in a third edition), a popular A level textbook.

Acknowledgements

All extracts from *Existentialism and Humanism* by Jean-Paul Sartre, translated by Philip Mairet, are reproduced by permission of Methuen Publishing Limited.

Extract on pages 23–4 from *Nausea* by Jean-Paul Sartre, translated by Robert Baldick, pp. 182–5, © Penguin Books Ltd, London, 1963, 1965. Reproduced by permission of Penguin Books Ltd.

First published in 2003
by John Murray (Publishers) Ltd, a member of the Hodder Headline Group
338 Euston Road
London NW1 3BH

Layouts by Fiona Webb
Artwork by Mike Humphries and Tony Randell
Cover design by John Townson/Creation
Cover photo courtesy of Mary Evans Picture Library

Typeset in 11/13pt Galliard by Dorchester Typesetting, Dorchester, Dorset
Printed and bound in Great Britain by Athenaeum Press Ltd, Gateshead, Tyne & Wear

A CIP catalogue record for this book is available from the British Library.

ISBN 0 7195 7188 X

Contents

Key to features

 A practical task to help you to understand Sartre's ideas.

▶ criticism ◀ Highlights and evaluates some of the difficulties Sartre faced.

 Plays around with some of the concepts discussed; looks at them from different angles.

 A direct quotation from one of Sartre's books.

 more difficult A more in-depth discussion of Sartre's work.

Read *E & H* pages Highlights the key pages of *Existentialism and Humanism* that you should read before continuing with this book.

The series

This is the first in a series of books aimed at students who are beginning to study philosophy. The books fill the 'middle ground' between introductory texts, which do not always provide enough detail to help students with their essays and examinations, and texts aimed at academics, which are often far too complex for new philosophy students to understand.

All of the study guides are written around the themes and texts for the AQA AS level philosophy specification. In addition to *Existentialism and Humanism: Jean-Paul Sartre* there are at least five more to be published:

- Plato's *Republic*
- Descartes' *Meditations*
- Epistemology: the Theory of Knowledge
- Philosophy of Religion
- Moral Philosophy.

The authors are writers with substantial experience of teaching philosophy at A Level. They are committed to making philosophy as accessible and engaging as possible, and so the study guides contain exercises to help students to grasp the philosophical theories and ideas that they will face.

Feedback and comments on these study guides would be welcome.

Notes on the text

This book is best used alongside *Existentialism and Humanism* although it can be read separately. The edition of *Existentialism and Humanism* to which we refer is the 1973 paperback Methuen publication translated by Philip Mairet. (We do not examine the translator's introduction there, pp. 5–19, or the discussion that follows, pp. 57–70.)

Because *Existentialism and Humanism* is a record of a lecture by Sartre, we use the words 'lecture' and 'text' interchangeably throughout this book.

We use the abbreviations *E & H* to refer to *Existentialism and Humanism* and *B & N* to refer to *Being and Nothingness*, Sartre's major account of existentialism.

Words in SMALL CAPITALS are explained in the Glossary on pages 126–30.

Introduction

This book examines a lecture given by one of the most famous philosophers of the last century, Jean-Paul Sartre (1905–80). Sartre was a leading proponent of the European movement of EXISTENTIALISM, and in the autumn of 1945 he gave a talk in defence of existentialism at the Club Maintenant in Paris. This lecture was eventually published in English as a small book called *Existentialism and Humanism* (abbreviated here to *E & H*). The main purpose of Sartre's existentialist philosophy was to show that we are absolutely free, but we spend most of our lives running away from this FREEDOM. In his lecture, Sartre seeks to defend existentialism against those critics who claim that his theory of freedom leads to selfishness and immorality. His argument in the lecture rests on showing that existentialism is a HUMANISM, in other words, that existentialism is a theory that finds value in human beings.

We want to look in some detail at the position taken by Sartre in his lecture, at his theory of existentialism and its implications, and at his argument that existentialism is a humanism. In order to do this we have not kept to the sequence of Sartre's ideas as he presented them in *E & H*. Most obviously, Sartre outlined the criticisms of his theory at the beginning of his lecture, whereas we deal with these at the end of our book. We have left them till last because, to appreciate them fully, we need first to understand Sartre's philosophy and its implications.

Overleaf is an outline of this book's approach to Sartre's theory.

Chapter 2   Outline of Sartre's life
            Context of E & H

Chapter 3   **Structure** of E & H:
            Table summarising the main themes and examples
            Diagram showing the structure of the lecture

Chapter 4   **Foundations** of Sartre's theory:
            Phenomenology
            Subjectivity
            Existence precedes essence
            Atheism
            Nothingness

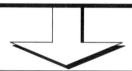

Implications of Sartre's theory:
Chapter 5   Metaphysical implications: Freedom and facticity
Chapter 6   Emotional implications: Abandonment, anguish and despair
Chapter 7   Ethical implications: Bad faith, authenticity and other people
Chapter 8   Ethical implications: Sartre's construction of an existentialist ethics

Chapter 9   **Criticisms** made against existentialism
            Sartre's defence against these criticisms
            Sartre's **conclusion** that existentialism is a humanism

Glossary
Selected bibliography

Background and context

Introduction

As with all philosophical works it is important to put *Existentialism and Humanism* into a historical context. Doing this does not mean that we have to dismiss it as out of date or no longer relevant, since we can still engage in a dialogue with Sartre's lecture, analyse it, defend it and add to it. However, knowing the historical context does help us to understand the focus of the work, why Sartre chose to emphasise this concept rather than that, and why he used this example rather than another. It also helps us to put the lecture in the context of Sartre's own development as a thinker; we begin to see it not as a polished final statement on existentialism, but as a stepping stone in his thoughts.

With this in mind the chapter is divided as follows:

- An outline of Sartre's life and works
- The background to *E & H*
- Some words of warning when reading the lecture
- Key points you need to know about the background and context of *E & H*.

You will notice that there are references to notes in this chapter and that these continue throughout the book. All of the notes appear on pages 131–6. Although following these up is not essential, they will give you the chance to do further research and to dig up more information for yourself.

An outline of Sartre's life and works

Jean-Paul Sartre was born in Paris in 1905. His father died in the same year, an event Sartre later saw as the most important event of his life as, in his own words, 'it gave me my freedom'.[1] Even as a boy Sartre displayed the characteristics of a hard-working intellectual: he had a thirst for reading; he wrote (and published) short stories; he even systematically recorded his own philosophical ideas in notebooks.

Sartre discovered philosophy whilst he was still at school and went on to to study it at the best university in France, the Ecole Normale Supérieure in Paris. Just before his final exams in 1929 he met a fellow philosopher and writer, Simone de

Beauvoir, and they agreed to experiment with an open relationship for the next few years (on Sartre's suggestion).[2] This relationship lasted their whole lives: they never married and never had children but long after they had ceased to be lovers they remained each other's closest friend and philosophical sparring partner.

When Sartre graduated he drifted into a teaching position in a provincial town, Le Havre, whilst de Beauvoir went south to a school in Marseilles. Sartre was an unorthodox schoolteacher, hating the discipline of it but enjoying making friends and hell-raising with his pupils. Sartre and de Beauvoir saw each other frequently and both established a habit of writing six hours a day, working on fiction and philosophy. Sartre remained a prolific writer for the rest of his life, assisted at times by amphetamines, which may have boosted his work-rate but did nothing for his readability.[3] In 1933 Sartre discovered the work of the German philosopher Husserl and obtained a grant to go to Berlin for a year, where he fell under the spell of not only the German PHENOMENOLOGISTS but also the wife of one of his colleagues. This was the first of many affairs that both Sartre and de Beauvoir were to have in their open relationship. He moved back to Paris to investigate his new ideas, and experimented in taking mescaline: the hallucinations that followed revealed a depth of hell in human consciousness that Sartre had never realised.[4] The effects were long-lasting, and for months Sartre felt the presence of giant lobsters which followed him along the streets. In the late 1930s Sartre wrote a flurry of philosophical works on consciousness, the emotions and the imagination, as well as short stories, published as *The Wall*, which conveyed his new way of thinking about the world. In 1938 he published his first novel, *Nausea*, based on his own experiences in Le Havre as a man whose life is transformed by a new awareness of his own EXISTENCE.

In 1939 Sartre was conscripted into the French army and in 1940, following the invasion and occupation of France by Germany, he found himself a prisoner of war in Germany. By posing as a civilian he managed to trick his way to freedom in 1941,[5] and he became part of a group of intellectuals committed to resisting the Nazis by using bulletins, rather than bullets.[6] He wrote some of his best works during the Second World War and these books and plays reveal Sartre's views on how we should live our lives. *No Exit* is a play about three people trapped in hell, with freedom an impossibility for them; his 'Roads To Freedom' trilogy traces the paths of a group of middle-class Parisians from the eve of the Second World War to the liberation of Paris. In 1943, during the German occupation, he published his most famous work of philosophy, *Being and Nothingness*, and by the end of the war he had become world renowned as a novelist, philosopher and playwright.

After the war his ideas and writings became increasingly popular in France, and Sartre found himself crowned as the 'Pope of Existentialism', with de Beauvoir known as 'Notre-Dame de Sartre'.[7] Sartre, de Beauvoir and their existential friends, such as Camus and Merleau-Ponty, were famous for their café culture, discussing politics and phenomenology whilst watching Parisian life go by.[8] But Sartre's ideas were already changing as he abandoned existentialism for a kind of Marxism. In 1964 he rejected the Nobel Prize for Literature on political grounds;[9] in 1967 he took part in the Russell Tribunal on American war crimes in Vietnam, with the 94-year-old British philosopher Bertrand Russell; and in May 1968 he was at the forefront of the student uprisings in Paris. Sartre said the very meaning of his life was to write,[10] and he led the kind of AUTHENTIC existence that he had always written about. He was a political activist on the front line of protest; he was a novelist and playwright committed to making his ideas engaging and accessible; he was a philosopher trying to make sense of his world. But through it all, as de Beauvoir said, he was someone who loved living.[11] He died in 1980, and at his funeral in Paris fifty thousand people, including de Beauvoir who was numb with grief, accompanied his body to the cemetery.

Sartre, like Marx before him, believed that it was the task of philosophy not only to interpret the world but also to change it.[12] Sartre wanted to transform people's lives, to convince us of our freedom and to show how, with commitment and energy, we can change our world. Sartre felt that this message was too important to be confined to universities and libraries. Unlike many philosophers he wanted everyone to be touched by his ideas and he used public lectures, newspaper articles, novels and plays to popularise his views. It was through Sartre's works of fiction that existentialism became best known: ANGST-ridden people chain-smoking in Parisian jazz clubs, the men wearing black polo-necks or goatee beards, and all expressing their existentialist freedom by doing whatever they wanted to do.[13] But there is more to existentialism than world-weary posing in cafés, as any brief glance at Sartre's huge work *Being and Nothingness* will show. Sartre genuinely wanted to transform people and to make us aware of the extent of our freedom. In this sense, then, existentialism is a journey, a kind of reawakening of consciousness. And it is a tough journey, as we experience nausea, ANGUISH and ABANDONMENT, until we finally reach liberation and an authentic existence.

The background to *Existentialism and Humanism*

Sartre gave his lecture *Existentialism and Humanism* a few months after the end of the Second World War. These were turbulent and depressing times: the extent of Nazi atrocities and the Holocaust was becoming clear to a horrified world; France was in turmoil as suspected collaborators of the Nazis were attacked, tried or executed; and a precarious alliance of nationalists and COMMUNISTS formed the French government led by Charles de Gaulle.

It was in this chaotic atmosphere that Sartre was asked to give a lecture explaining and defending his theory of existentialism.[14] On the evening of 29 October 1945, Sartre walked from the subway to the Club Maintenant, which had been hired for the occasion, and was confronted by hordes of people bustling round the entrance. At first he thought they had come to protest against him, but then realised they were trying to squeeze into the crowded building. Sartre did not want to draw attention to himself, and so was pushed and shoved around as he made his way to the platform at the front of the hall.

The lecture itself was a boisterous and noisy affair. Sartre, hands in pockets, spoke without notes to the packed hall. The atmosphere was claustrophobic, people fainted in the heat, chairs were broken and the police were called. Eventually Sartre stopped speaking – he had no more to say, he had run out of time for debate – and so he just left. The next day he was a celebrity, his name appearing in many newspapers as the leader of the new movement called existentialism. This tag remained with him for the rest of his life.

Some words of warning when reading the lecture

To make the task of understanding Sartre slightly easier, it is worth taking into account the following five points when reading the lecture.

■ The lecture should really be called 'Existentialism is a humanism'

The title of the lecture in the most common English version, as translated by Philip Mairet, is *Existentialism and Humanism*. But this title does not capture the full meaning of what the lecture was all about. The actual French title, as announced in the newspaper advertising Sartre's lecture, was *L'Existentialisme est un humanisme*, which means

'Existentialism is a humanism'. This is more accurate as it describes the main thrust of Sartre's lecture, which was a defence of existentialism against those who wanted to claim that it is *not* a type of humanism.[15]

What is humanism? In its most general sense 'humanism' represents the tendency to treat human affairs as of prime concern and value. It takes humans, rather than God, to be the centre of interest.[16] In the Renaissance, many scholars, philosophers and artists were humanists, whilst still believing that God the creator existed. By the time Sartre was writing, humanism was associated with ATHEISM and had taken on a moral slant. This ethical humanism held that humans needed to work out for themselves their moral values, without the guidance of traditional authorities or of God. So, for Sartre to claim that existentialism is a kind of humanism is to say that existentialism values humanity even in the absence of God.

Above all, the lecture is an attempt by Sartre to persuade his critics that existentialism is not a vicious, selfish or anarchic philosophy which allows everyone to do what they like. Sartre claims that an existentialist MORALITY is possible, and so *E & H* can be seen both as an outline of his theory of existentialism and as a sketch of his moral philosophy.

Sartre abbreviates and simplifies his ideas

As an outline of existentialism Sartre's lecture is deceptively simple. His time for speaking to the audience was limited, and he wanted to make many points in defence of existentialism. Sartre was also speaking to an audience familiar with his theory and so he does not bother to explain all his ideas as he speaks. Thus we find that many of his key ideas are missing from the lecture or are given short shrift. In order for us to understand his lecture more fully, we shall need to look at what is missing from it, and at what lies behind the concepts he casually drops into it. In particular we shall have to draw on his weighty book, *Being and Nothingness.*

The simplicity of the lecture may also be due to Sartre's attitude to philosophy. We have already noted that, for Sartre, philosophy is not merely an activity for professors in ivory towers but is something that affects all of us. With this lecture Sartre was trying to extend his philosophy to the widest possible audience, and it is very much an attempt to win over his listeners to existentialism. To offer complex philosophical explanations and arguments would not have helped his cause and, in any case, rigorous proof was not Sartre's style. As philosopher Mary Warnock said: 'A proof is, [for Sartre], a description so clear and vivid that, when I think of this description and apply it to my own case, I cannot fail to see its application.'[17]

The lack of considered argument is made up for by Sartre's passion for his ideas and by the many striking and memorable examples he uses. So, it is important to dig deeper into the lecture in order to expose Sartre's philosophical ideas and arguments. Again, this means that we shall have to explore some of Sartre's other philosophical works and notebooks.

■ **The message of Sartre's lecture was influenced by the situation in France**

Sartre's lecture had a deep significance and resonance in post-war France. His country had been occupied by the Germans for nearly six years but was finally liberated and had a sense of starting over again. Sartre was delivering his message of freedom and responsibility against a background of reprisals and attacks on collaborators. This affected his choice of examples in the lecture, many of which revolve around the painful decisions people face in wartime. It also influenced the passion with which he expresses his beliefs. For Sartre, we can never blame anyone else for the way we ourselves have acted. If we have actively collaborated with the Nazis and overseen the deaths of our neighbours, then we cannot blame our circumstances; we must take responsibility. In the same way, if we have ignored the Nazi occupation and have continued as if life had not changed, then we must take responsibility for that as well. Sartre's assertion of the absolute responsibility for action can be felt on nearly every page of the text.

■ **The lecture is not Sartre's definitive statement on existentialism or on ethics**

Although *Existentialism and Humanism* is one of the most widely read and popular of Sartre's works, we must note that, for Sartre himself, it had only a minor place within his philosophy. The huge philosophical texts that he wrote before and after the lecture (*Being and Nothingness*, 1943, and *Critique of Dialectical Reason*, 1960) make no reference to the new ideas contained in the lecture. In particular, Sartre ignored in his later published work the ETHICAL substance of the lecture, which seems so central when we first read it.

Although Sartre did give the lecture once more (in private, so that there could be a discussion without all the heckling) and allowed it to be published in 1946, he never followed up the lecture with a book giving a more sustained exploration of his new thoughts. Sartre was constantly rethinking his ideas and reshaping them into new theories, which he kept in notebooks and presented in talks around the world. Sartre's *Notebooks for an Ethics*, published after his death, show that his ideas on an existentialist ethical theory were continually developing. Later in his life he rejected *E & H* and regretted the fact that many saw it as the clearest statement of his ideas. So, once again, we should be warned that this lecture, which has become the most popular book to read on existentialism, is not a definitive summary of Sartre's position.

■ Sartre has a special way with words

Despite his desire to make his ideas widespread, Sartre's philosophical writings are often very inaccessible, and *E & H* is no exception. There are many reasons why Sartre's works are so difficult to understand, apart from the complexity of the subject matter. He seems to use words (such as 'anguish' or 'despair') in his own special way, and he is not always consistent in his definition of them. He invents words when he needs to, and he adds hyphens all over the place to create new concepts. He uses lots of metaphors and quirky or paradoxical turns of phrase.[18] He sometimes says that he is defining words when he is actually introducing new ideas. His train of thought, particularly in the lecture, is not always clear as, in his passion for his beliefs, he jumps from one idea to the next. This lack of clarity is made worse for English-speaking readers by the fact that they are reading a translation. To help to make sense of some of Sartre's ideas we have provided a Glossary of his terminology at the end of this book (see pages 126–30).

We should note here the meaning of one crucial word – value – which Sartre uses throughout the lecture. By this term he tends to mean moral or ethical values as opposed to other kinds of value. We have followed him in this convention, and when we talk about value in this book we are generally referring to ethical values. We shall see later that the origin of values is a central issue for Sartre.

One other point to make about Sartre's use of language is his tendency to talk about 'man' and 'mankind'. This was the convention then, but, despite his close relationship with one of the world's leading feminists, de Beauvoir, it is possible that Sartre really was thinking only of men when he spoke of 'man's freedom'.[19] We have used the words 'human' and 'humanity', instead of 'man' and 'mankind', wherever possible.

experimenting with ideas

1 Read the 'Existentialist Fast-Stream' questionnaire overleaf. This assesses whether you have the sort of personality that is conducive to existentialism, and whether you are ready to enter the fast-track to freedom.

2 Using a blank piece of paper, record your answers.

EXISTENTIALIST FAST-STREAM

IN CONFIDENCE

Thank you for your interest in joining the Existentialist Fast-Stream. In order for us to assess your suitability for this position we require you to complete the psychometric test below. The information that you give here will be used to assist with the decision to invite you to the next stage of the selection process. Providing false or misleading information may disqualify your candidature.

1 How would you describe yourself? *Choose* **four** *of the following*:

Rebellious   Creative   Confident   Helpful   Independent   Active
Organised   Careful   Patient   Responsible   Laid back   Philosophical

2 I find that . . . *Circle* **one** *number in each row.*

	Much less often than most of my friends	**A bit less** often than most of my friends	About the **same** as most of my friends	**A bit more** often than most of my friends	**Much more** often than most of my friends
a) I think about others when I act	1	2	3	4	5
b) I worry about my future	1	2	3	4	5
c) I spend a lot of time doing nothing	1	2	3	4	5
d) I know what role to play in social situations	1	2	3	4	5
e) I tend to take chances	1	2	3	4	5
f) I change my image	1	2	3	4	5
g) I do what I want to do	1	2	3	4	5
h) I question conventional assumptions	1	2	3	4	5

3 In which of the following areas do you consider yourself to be strongest and weakest? *Pick only* **one** *area as the strongest, and* **one** *area as the weakest.*

	Strongest	**Weakest**
a) Achieving what I set out to achieve		
b) Changing bad habits		
c) Doing what I'm supposed to do		
d) Knowing what I want from life		
e) Making difficult decisions		

4 Choose **six** of the following activities. *Circle* **six** *letters only.*

a) Having a cigarette
b) Standing on a chair
c) Drawing on a board
d) Tidying up
e) Telling someone a dream
f) Having a philosophical discussion with a teacher
g) Reading out loud
h) Closing your eyes

i) Scrunching up paper and playing basketball with it
j) Jogging
k) Finding chalk
l) Quoting Shakespeare
m) Speaking in French
n) Planning a day out for 16 underprivileged children
o) Miming your favourite film
p) Telling jokes

5 If you could change anything about your personality what would you choose to change?

6 If you could choose to do anything what would you choose to do?
You should continue on a separate piece of paper if necessary.

ACTIVITY   Look at the answers you have written for the 'Existentialist Fast-Stream'
            questionnaire. Now answer these additional questions, related to
            each one in the questionnaire.

1 Will you always possess these qualities? Which ones will change?
   Why?
2 Are any of these inconsistent with the characteristics you chose in
   Question 1?
3 Was this true of you ten years ago?
4 How did you make those choices?
5 How might you go about changing this?
6 What is stopping you from doing it?

▨ Analysis of the questionnaire

The questionnaire you have just answered is an imitation of a
kind of test known as 'psychometric'. This is designed to
assess your personality, and sometimes employers such as the
Civil Service use it to check your suitability for a job.

Sartre would see such personality tests as dangerous
because they encourage us to think of ourselves as having an
'inner self' which never changes and which determines our
behaviour. Even more ridiculous to Sartre would be the idea
of a test for an 'existentialist' type of person. The most he
might have said was that you could 'pass' the test only if you
refused to do it, or threw it away. This is because he believed
that no one has a fixed personality that makes them a
particular type of person. Instead, Sartre believed that we are
all free to change our character, and our life, as we choose.

Sartre's lecture, *E & H*, attempts to show why we are free
and what we should do with this freedom. In the next chapter
we shall sketch out the basic argument that Sartre gives in his
lecture.

Key points: Chapter 2

What you need to know about the **background and context** of *E & H*:

1 Sartre was a philosopher committed to changing the way we think and act.

2 Sartre wanted his ideas to be accessible to as many people as possible. His lectures, novels and plays were all vehicles for his philosophical message.

3 The text *Existentialism and Humanism* is a record of a lecture Sartre gave just after the end of the Second World War.

4 The lecture should really be called 'Existentialism is a humanism'. This more accurately captures the main theme of the lecture (that existentialism is a form of humanist philosophy).

5 In the lecture, Sartre abbreviates many important parts of his theory so that he can expand on other parts. He also simplifies his ideas to make them more accessible to his audience.

6 The message of Sartre's lecture was affected by the situation in post-war France. Many people were blaming others for the horrors that had taken place, but Sartre tells his audience that everyone must take responsibility.

7 The lecture is not Sartre's definitive statement on existentialism or on ethics. Two years before the lecture, Sartre had written *Being and Nothingness* which is his most definitive account of existentialism. After the lecture, Sartre struggled in his notebooks to combine existentialism with a more ethical philosophy. His final philosophical writings move away from existentialism almost completely. So, the lecture is best seen as a stepping stone in Sartre's own philosophical journey.

8 Sartre has a special way with words. In the lecture, and in his other writings, Sartre uses words in unusual ways. Often he does not provide a clear definition of his terms, and sometimes the meaning is lost in the translation from French to English. There are two popular translations of the lecture into English (the Mairet translation to which we refer throughout this book and the Baskin translation in *Sartre: Essays in Existentialism*, Citadel Press, 1993). You may find it helpful to use both in order to get a better understanding of what Sartre is trying to say.

Structure of *Existentialism and Humanism*

Introduction

We have seen that *Existentialism and Humanism* is a record of a lecture that Sartre gave in post-war Paris. He gave the talk without notes and the structure of the lecture is not at all clear. The published text, which is based on the talk, is therefore one continuous piece of prose, punctuated by the occasional paragraph break. The fact that there are few obvious signposts to guide the reader can make it difficult to follow the flow of Sartre's argument.

In this chapter we have broken down the lecture into five sections to make it easier to understand his argument. You may find different or additional sections. Our choice is as follows:

1 Attack on existentialism
2 Foundations of existentialism
3 Implications of existentialism
4 Defence of existentialism
5 Conclusion.

Our section-by-section breakdown of *E & H* consists of two summaries. The first summary (pages 14–18) is in the form of a table that indicates where the main themes and ideas occur and this should help to highlight the connections between the chapters in this book and Sartre's text. The second summary (page 19) is a diagram which shows the 'flow' of Sartre's argument and which simplifies the structure of the lecture even further. So, this chapter is divided into three sections:

■ A table summarising the content of *E & H*
■ A diagram showing the structure of *E & H*
■ Key points you need to know about the structure of *E & H*.

ACTIVITY
1 Read the table (pages 14–18) and the diagram (page 19).
2 On slips of paper, write the sections and main headings throughout the lecture. Put these bookmarks in your copy of *E & H* to help you to make sense of it later on.
3 Now spend two hours reading the text of *E & H*. You may not understand much of it at this point but the more times you read it, the clearer it will become.

Summary of Existentialism and Humanism

Section	Page*	Summary	Themes explored	Examples used
1 Attack on existentialism	23	*Introduction to the text* In the first sentence Sartre clearly states his intention: to defend existentialism against some of the criticisms made against it. Given the title of the lecture, this suggests his critics are saying that existentialism is not a humanism; Sartre thinks he can show that existentialism is a humanism.		
	23	*Criticism A: Existentialism is pessimistic* Some people (especially communists) have argued that existentialism leads people away from positive action and that, instead, it encourages inaction – the QUIETISM of DESPAIR' – and contemplation, which is a luxury of the middle classes.	■ The criticisms laid against existentialism	
	23	*Criticism B: Existentialism emphasises the uglier side of life* Some, for example Christians, say that existentialism focuses on all that is 'mean, sordid or base' about life (this point is repeated on p. 24). They say it ignores the beauty of life, such as the smile of a baby.	■ The criticisms laid against existentialism	■ The smile of a baby
	23	*Criticism C: Existentialism isolates individuals* Communists also say that existentialism ignores the solidarity of humanity, the common connection that we all have with each other. The implication is that existentialism focuses only on the selfish position of the individual.	■ The criticisms laid against existentialism	
	23–4	*Criticism D: Existentialism is an amoral theory* Christians also argue that existentialists are denying the existence of morality because they deny God's existence. For existentialists, it seems as if we can do whatever we want to do, without being condemned, as there are no 'eternal' moral values.	■ The criticisms laid against existentialism	
	24–5	*Defence against Criticism B: Existentialism is not as depressing as common wisdom* Existentialist writing is no more ugly or evil than other 'naturalistic' novels, such as those by Emile Zola. Much more depressing than existentialism are the old sayings that tell us to stay in our place and do nothing. Existentialism is actually really positive, in its emphasis on the possibility of freedom.	■ The responses to those criticisms	

Section	Page*	Summary	Themes explored	Examples used
2 Foundations of existentialism: An introduction to the theory of existentialism	25–7	*Existence precedes essence* What does 'existentialism' mean? Sartre tries to explain existentialism to his audience, without referring to the complex ideas of *Being and Nothingness*. Sartre says that all existentialists begin from the SUBJECTIVE, or from the belief that, for humans, existence comes before ESSENCE. His example of the paperknife illustrates what it means for something to have an essence before it exists – it must have been designed, with specific materials and use already in the mind of the designer.	■ EXISTENCE PRECEDES ESSENCE ■ The nature of human reality, in contrast with that of material objects	■ The paperknife is designed (has an essence) before it is made (has an existence)
	27–8	*Atheism* Many people believe that humans have an essence (or purpose) which has been decided upon prior to their existence, and they also believe in some kind of 'divine craftsman' – a God. Even those philosophers who do not believe that God designed humans still cling on to the belief that humans have an essence – a 'HUMAN NATURE'. But Sartre says that only atheistic existentialists are consistent in both denying God's existence and denying human nature.	■ God and human nature ■ The rejection of DETERMINISM	■ Immanuel Kant's idea that all humans have an essence (even the bourgeois and the wild man of the woods share fundamental qualities)
	28–9	*Subjectivity* This section identifies a further foundation of existentialism – subjectivity. For Sartre, a subjective life is one that is free. Subjects invent themselves as they live, making choices, defining themselves only through their actions, and reinventing themselves. This is not the case with plants, as they lack subjectivity. Our subjectivity is intimately connected with our freedom.	■ The rejection of determinism ■ The nature of human reality, in contrast with that of material objects	■ Man is a project with a subjective life ■ Moss, fungi and cauliflowers do not possess a subjective life
3 Implications of existentialism: Metaphysical, Emotional, Ethical	28–9	*Metaphysical implications: Freedom* Here, Sartre goes overboard in his enthusiasm for human freedom. Although he says 'man is nothing', unlike in *Being and Nothingness* Sartre does not base this freedom on 'NOTHINGNESS'. He assumes that if our existence precedes our essence, if there is no God, if we begin with subjectivity, then we are free. What follows from our freedom is that we alone must accept responsibility for our choices.	■ Freedom, choice and responsibility	■ Comparing humans to a stone, a table or a kind of moss
	29–30	*Ethical implications 1: defence against criticism D* Sartre introduces the main theme of the lecture: that existentialism does consider other people. (If Sartre can show that existentialism does value humans, then he is right to say that existentialism is a humanism.) Sartre's argument is sketchy here, but basically he is saying: there are no values except those we choose. But what we value (for example, getting married) is always something we think other people should value, and so what we choose is always something we think other people should choose. As choice brings with it responsibility, we are therefore responsible for everyone who makes the same choices we make.	■ Freedom, choice and responsibility ■ Relation of choice to value ■ Sartre's use of universalisation ■ The implication for morality	■ Choosing a Christian, not a communist trade union ■ Choosing to get married ■ Choosing to have children

Summary of Existentialism and Humanism

Section	Page*	Summary	Themes explored	Examples used
3 Implications of existentialism: Metaphysical, Emotional, Ethical	30–2	*Emotional implications 1: Anguish and responsibility* What happens when we realise we are free? How do we react to our freedom? Anguish is the feeling we have when we understand that we are responsible not only for our own choices but also for everyone else's! This global responsibility cannot be avoided, even if we say 'God told me to do this', or 'A voice told me to do this' or 'I was ordered to do this', because we could always have ignored God or the voice or the order. It was our choice to listen and obey, and so we must accept responsibility for our actions.	▓ Freedom, choice and responsibility ▓ Why man's situation gives rise to anguish ▓ The existentialist meaning of anguish	▓ Abraham choosing to sacrifice his son ▓ The woman who chooses to hear voices as God ▓ The military leader who chooses to follow an order and send his troops to their death
	32–9	*Emotional implications 2: Abandonment and choice* The second emotional implication is abandonment. This begins with the realisation that God does not exist. Some philosophers have accepted this, but tried to replace God with other kinds of OBJECTIVE values. They are mistaken. Only the existentialist realises fully that if there is no God, then there can be no objective values and no human nature. Humans are free to do anything, and have no guide or rules to help them, and must invent themselves. There can be no excuses for our actions – we alone are responsible for them, and thus responsible for all humanity. (This has already been mentioned on pp. 29–30.) It is no good asking others for advice, or blaming our actions on our emotions, or looking for hidden signs in the world. We choose all of these things: whom we ask for advice; which emotions we follow; how we interpret a 'sign'. Choice is an unavoidable consequence of abandonment.	▓ The rejection of determinism ▓ Freedom, choice and responsibility ▓ Why man's situation gives rise to abandonment ▓ The existentialist meaning of abandonment	▓ The attack on objective values ▓ Dostoyevsky's quote ▓ Sartre's pupil, the central dilemma of the lecture: should he look after his mother, or join the resistance? ▓ Asking advice from a priest ▓ The Jesuit who saw his failures as a sign
	39–42	*Emotional implications 3: Despair and quietism* The third of the emotional consequences is despair. Living in despair means facing up to the fact that our actions are limited and there is no God who can help us out beyond those limits. There is no point worrying about things that are beyond our control, or hoping that somehow, by the intervention of God, our situation will be altered to become what we want it to be. If something is beyond our control, we should not concern ourselves with it. However, this does not mean that we should stop acting just because we have no control over what happens when we die. That is quietism, and it goes against the existential belief that action is everything. After all, we are nothing except the sum of our actions. Our actions make us what we are. So, we must reject quietism. Nor must we blame our life on other things, such as our past, as that also leads to quietism (giving up on action). We are free to try to alter our circumstances. We are what we choose to do.	▓ Why man's situation gives rise to despair ▓ The existentialist meaning of despair	▓ Hoping that the train comes on time ▓ Worrying about what will happen after our death ▓ Blaming our life on our circumstances – 'everything was against me' ▓ The genius of Proust is the works of Proust

Section	Page*	Summary	Themes explored	Examples used
4 Defence of existentialism	42–4	*Defence against criticism A: Existentialism is optimistic* Sartre returns to his defence of existentialism. From all that we have read we can see that existentialism is not pessimistic. Sartre's novels are not pessimistic because the characters are free to choose, and if they end up doing horrible things, it is by their own choice, not because they are determined by their environment or heredity (as in Zola's books). We are totally in control of what we do, and responsible for what we do – this is a very optimistic theory. We were not born a COWARD, but we become a coward through our cowardly actions, and this means that we can change and become a hero through our heroic actions. Sartre's theory is optimistic because it places our destiny in our hands, it reveals that we control all our actions and hence our lives, and it rejects inaction (or quietism).	■ Rejection of determinism ■ Authenticity ■ The responses to the criticisms	■ Zola blaming behaviour on upbringing ■ The coward becomes a coward by his actions
	44–7	*Defence against criticism C: Existentialism unites individuals* Existentialism is based on the only point of certainty available to humans: Descartes' COGITO. This is what Sartre calls the 'subjectivity of the individual', and it means 'I am aware of myself, I am self-conscious'. Any theory based on any other so-called truths lacks strong foundations. However, just because existentialism begins with the individual subject it does not mean it isolates the individual. We need other people in order to recognise ourselves as a self-conscious being. Other people make us aware of what kind of being we are, so our subjectivity depends on everyone else's subjectivity. This is INTERSUBJECTIVITY. Also, just because Sartre has rejected human nature, this does not mean there is nothing in common between humans. In fact, we all share certain limitations (FACTICITY), the same lived experience (the human condition) and, most importantly, the same freedom and commitment to freedom. So, existentialism goes beyond the individual subject and does consider others.	■ Subjectivism, the cogito, intersubjectivity ■ Authenticity ■ The responses to the criticisms	■ Our historical situations may vary, but we share the same fundamental situation ■ Every purpose, and goal, can be understood around the world
	47–53	*Ethical implications 2: Defence against criticism D* Sartre feels that he needs to go further in proving that existentialism considers others. He reminds us again that we are responsible for choosing for everyone, and this choice is unavoidable. But this morality is not based on any objective values, instead it is created like the work of an artist. Just as artists invent and create a work of art through their choices, so we invent and create our morality through our choices. Does this mean that moral judgements are impossible, because it is all a matter of personal opinion? Sartre says that we can make a judgement about morality – namely, whether our choices are authentic (based on the truth of our freedom) or whether they are based on the false idea that we are not free. So, Sartre's judgements are 'logical' rather than 'moral'. He attacks those people he thinks of as self-deceivers; people who pretend they are not free are lying to themselves. Sartre	■ Authenticity and self-deception (bad faith) ■ The responses to the criticisms ■ Freedom, choice and responsibility ■ The possibility of moral criticism ■ The implications for morality	■ The attack on Gide ■ Moral choice is like the construction of a work of art ■ The self-deceiver is in error ■ Cowards and SCUM

Summary of Existentialism and Humanism

Section	Page*	Summary	Themes explored	Examples used
4 Defence of existentialism	47–53 (contd.)	then puts forward a second version of his existential morality. He says that when we make a choice we are actually choosing freedom. And so we choose freedom for all humanity. Those self-deceivers (in BAD FAITH) who deny this are either scum, who think their existence is necessary, or cowards, who run away from their freedom. Freedom, then, is now at the heart of Sartre's existential morality.		
5 Conclusion: existentialism is a humanism	53–6	*Conclusion: Existentialism is a humanism* Sartre believes that moral values lie in our choices, whatever those choices are. The important thing is that our choices are made in the knowledge that we are free. Sartre, having defended existentialism against the criticisms made against it, now says that existentialism is a humanism. It is not a humanism that values people just because they are human, as that leads to fascism. Instead, existentialism is a humanism that values the potential of people to be free, to make choices, to invent morality. Finally, Sartre admits that the existence or non-existence of God makes no difference to his theory.	■ The responses to the criticisms	■ Maggie Tulliver and La Sanseverina ■ 'Man is magnificent' ■ The cult of humanity

*See *Existentialism and Humanism* (trans. Philip Mairet), Methuen, 1973.

The structure of *Existentialism and Humanism*

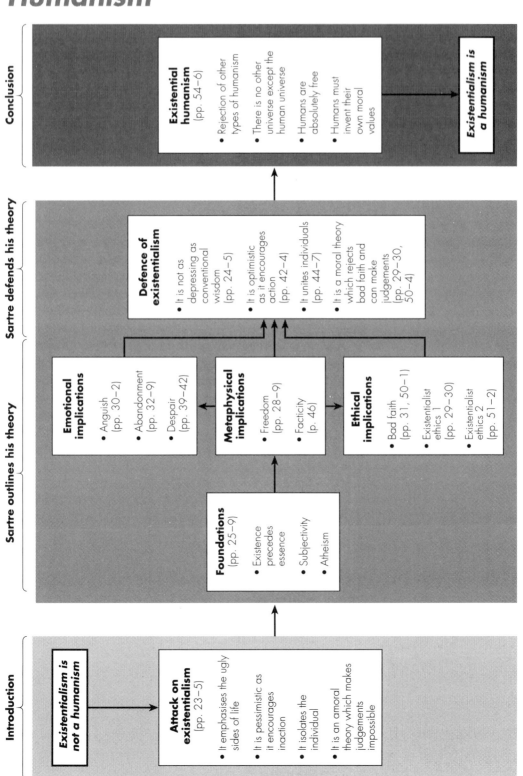

Introduction

Existentialism is not a humanism

Attack on existentialism (pp. 23–5)
- It emphasises the ugly sides of life
- It is pessimistic as it encourages inaction
- It isolates the individual
- It is an amoral theory which makes judgements impossible

Sartre outlines his theory

Foundations (pp. 25–9)
- Existence precedes essence
- Subjectivity
- Atheism

Emotional implications
- Anguish (pp. 30–2)
- Abandonment (pp. 32–9)
- Despair (pp. 39–42)

Metaphysical implications
- Freedom (pp. 28–9)
- Facticity (p. 46)

Ethical implications
- Bad faith (pp. 31, 50–1)
- Existentialist ethics 1 (pp. 29–30)
- Existentialist ethics 2 (pp. 51–2)

Sartre defends his theory

Defence of existentialism
- It is not as depressing as conventional wisdom (pp. 24–5)
- It is optimistic as it encourages action (pp. 42–4)
- It unites individuals (pp. 44–7)
- It is a moral theory which rejects bad faith and can make judgements (pp. 29–30, 50–4)

Conclusion

Existential humanism (pp. 54–6)
- Rejection of other types of humanism
- There is no other universe except the human universe
- Humans are absolutely free
- Humans must invent their own moral values

Existentialism is a humanism

Key points: Chapter 3

What you need to know about the **structure** of *E & H*:

1 Sartre did not clearly divide his lecture into sections and subsections, but it is possible to see the lecture as divided into sections.

2 We see the lecture as structured into five main sections:

- Sartre outlines the attacks made against his theory (pages 23–5)
- Sartre outlines the foundations of his theory (pages 25–9)
- Sartre draws out the implications of his theory (pages 28–42)
- Sartre defends his theory against the attacks (pages 42–54)
- Sartre concludes his lecture (pages 54–6).

3 However, these sections are artificially drawn. There is some overlap between the sections, and items from one section (for example, his defence against the claim that existentialism is not a moral theory) can be found in other sections.

4 We recommend that you go through your copy of *E & H* and try to identify the section headings that you feel make sense. Write these on bookmarks (slips of paper or Post-It notes).

Foundations of Sartre's existentialism

Introduction

Read E & H pages 25–9

We have mentioned that Sartre simplified and compressed his ideas in the lecture. This oversimplification in *Existentialism and Humanism* can lead people to conclude that Sartre's arguments are incredibly weak. Knowing his position in more detail will help us to defend him against at least some of the more basic criticisms laid against him. So, to arrive at a full understanding of the views put forward in *E & H*, we must first be clear about the concepts that underpin Sartre's existentialism.

In this chapter we are going to look at the philosophical method that Sartre uses and at the foundations of his theory. The foundations are those that we have gleaned from what Sartre said, both in *E & H* and in his most comprehensive existentialist work, *Being and Nothingness (B & N)*. The chapter is divided as follows:

- Sartre's method: Phenomenology
- The foundations of Sartre's theory
- Foundation 1: Subjectivity and the *cogito*
- Foundation 2: Existence precedes essence
- Foundation 3: Atheism
- Foundation 4: Nothingness
- Key points you need to know about the foundations of Sartre's existentialism.

Sartre's method: Phenomenology

In both his fiction and his philosophy Sartre draws heavily on a philosophical method called phenomenology. So, if we are to understand the approach that Sartre takes in *Existentialism and Humanism*, it would help if we had some understanding of phenomenology.

We can begin by saying that phenomenology is one way amongst many of doing philosophy. Philosophers disagree with each other about most things; we might say that it is a part of their job. One of the things they disagree about is the best way of doing philosophy; in other words, they disagree over a philosophical method (this is not the case with most academic subjects). Rationalists, for example, believe that the best way of seeking the truth is to use reason, whilst empiricists say that we should draw on our experience alone. Sartre, at the beginning of his philosophical career, discovered and began to use a method known as phenomenology. This approach was founded in the early 1900s by the German philosopher Husserl and was popularised by Heidegger in the 1920s and 1930s. When Sartre went to do some research in Germany, in 1933, he started to use phenomenology in his own particular way, and this method of examining the world influenced both his philosophy and his fiction.

What does phenomenology mean? Literally it is the study (-ology) of appearances (phenomena): the world as it appears in our consciousness. Some examples of 'phenomena' might be the colour of this page, or the sounds you are hearing right now, or your feelings of stress as you struggle to pronounce 'phenomenology'. These are the sensations that furnish your mind. Later in this chapter (page 29), you will have the opportunity to take a phenomenological approach to your own life.

Philosophers who take a phenomenological approach claim that studying the experiences of the conscious mind is all that we can really ever do, and that those experiences are all that we can ever really know. They say that, because of this, phenomenology is the best and only way of approaching philosophy. Why do some philosophers make such a radical claim?

experimenting with ideas

1 Imagine losing your senses one by one. Take away sight, sound, touch, etc. What would you still be aware of?

2 Now imagine you were not conscious at all. What would the world be like for you?

From the Activity you will see that there is a very close relationship between our world, our senses and our consciousness. If we lose our senses, or our consciousness, then our world ceases to exist.

A phenomenologist might argue that all we know about the world is what appears to the conscious mind: the colours, the shapes, the sounds, the noises, the feelings, and so on. It is from these building blocks that, as children, we start to construct a complex picture of the world, of how all these objects of consciousness fit together to form an 'external reality'. Thus, phenomenology seeks to explore the world by looking at how the conscious mind perceives it, since for us this is how the world comes to be. A phenomenologist says that we must limit our philosophical investigations to what we, as conscious beings, are aware of.

A phenomenological approach is very different from empiricism, even though both methods seem to start with our experiences. Phenomenology takes our consciousness, its activity and objects, as the beginning and end of philosophy: we are not trying to extrapolate from our experiences to what the world is 'really like' out there. Phenomenologists believe that we should forget about ('put into brackets') things existing outside of us, and instead concentrate on describing and analysing our mental activities. Some, such as Husserl, further believed that by bracketing the world and analysing only phenomena we might even reach some understanding of the essential nature of things.

The attraction of phenomenology is that we can do it anywhere! De Beauvoir recalls the moment when Sartre first heard about phenomenology from their friend Aron: 'Aron said, pointing to his glass: "You see, my dear fellow, if you are a phenomenologist, you can talk about this cocktail and make a philosophy out of it"'.[20] Sartre's own phenomenological approach is best illustrated by an extract from one of his novels, *Nausea*.

ACTIVITY   Read the extract below from Sartre's novel *Nausea*. The main character, Roquentin, is keeping a diary which records the feelings of nausea that he has started to have.

1 What do you think Sartre is trying to say in this passage?
2 How does this extract differ from other pieces of philosophy that you may have read?
3 In what way does the extract illustrate a 'phenomenological' approach?

I was in the municipal park just now. The root of the chestnut tree plunged into the ground just underneath my bench. I no longer remembered that it was a root. Words had disappeared, and with them the meaning of things, the methods of using them, the feeble landmarks which men have traced on their surface. I was sitting, slightly bent, my head bowed, alone in front of that black, knotty mass, which was utterly crude and frightened me. And then I had this revelation.

It took my breath away. Never, until these last few days, had I suspected what it meant to 'exist'. I was like the others, like those who walk along the seashore in their spring clothes. I used to say like them: 'The sea is green; that white speck up there is a seagull', but I didn't feel that it existed, that the seagull was an 'existing seagull'; usually existence hides itself. It is there, around us, in us, it is us, you can't say a couple of words without speaking of it, but finally you can't touch it . . . And then all of a sudden, there it was, as clear as day: existence had suddenly unveiled itself. It had lost its harmless appearance as an abstract category: it was the very stuff of things, that root was steeped in existence. Or rather the root, the park gates, the bench, the sparse grass on the lawn, all that had vanished; the diversity of things, their individuality, was only an appearance, a veneer. This veneer had melted, leaving soft monstrous masses, in disorder – naked, with a frightening, obscene nakedness . . .

All those objects . . . how can I explain? They embarrassed me; I would have liked them to exist less strongly, in a drier, more abstract way, with more reserve. The chestnut tree pressed itself against my eyes. Green rust covered it halfway up; the bark, black and blistered, looked like boiled leather. The soft sound of the water in the Masqueret Fountain flowed into my ears and made a nest there, filling them with sighs; my nostrils overflowed with a green, putrid smell . . . Superfluous: that was the only connection I could establish between those trees, those gates, those pebbles. It was in vain that I tried to count the chestnut trees, to situate them in relation to the Velleda, to compare their height with the height of the plane trees: each of them escaped from the relationship in which I tried to enclose it, isolated itself, overflowed. I was aware of the arbitrary nature of these relationships, which I insisted on maintaining in order to delay the collapse of the human world of measures, of quantities, of bearing; they no longer had any grip on things. Superfluous, the chestnut tree, over there, opposite me, a little to the left. Superfluous, the Velleda . . . And I . . . I too was superfluous. (Nausea, *pp. 182–5)*

The character Roquentin may appear to be losing his mind a little here, but what does this passage tell us about Sartre's method – his way of doing philosophy? For Sartre, our analysis of the world must begin with our experiences and we cannot escape this fact. Using a phenomenological method, Sartre not only analyses what consciousness is but also investigates our emotions, our feelings, our experiences/sense data as sources of information that throw light on to our existence. Sartre uses examples in his works that many philosophers would dismiss: the feelings of nausea when confronted with the enormity of the world; the DISGUST at material objects or our bodies; the feeling we get when we are watched; or the experience of looking out for a friend in a crowd of people. These closely observed descriptions of our inner lives occur in both his fiction and his philosophy; but it is crucial to Sartre that he has enabled us, the readers, to recognise in the example something (some phenomenon) that we have experienced ourselves. His descriptions 'click' with us, and we understand what he is talking about.

▶ criticism ◀ As a philosopher who uses phenomenology, Sartre relies upon illustrations, rather than arguments, in order to convince us of his ideas. This has led philosophers from a more 'analytic' tradition to criticise him for his lack of clear argument. The English philosopher Mary Warnock wrote of Sartre's method:[21]

'Philosophically speaking there is a difference between a description (however vivid) and proof. The novelist or the film director need not observe the differences, but a philosopher must. It is the death of philosophy if it confuses the true with the convincing.'

ACTIVITY

1 Read the quotation from Mary Warnock. What criticism do you think she is making of Sartre?

2 From your initial reading of E & H, do you think the lecture has more:
   a) arguments/proofs
   b) descriptions/examples?

3 Imagine you are justifying one of your most strongly held beliefs in a philosophy class. Use a table like this to record the advantages and disadvantages of the two methods of supporting your views:

	Using an argument or proof to support my belief	Using a persuasive description or example to support my belief
Advantages		
Disadvantages		

The foundations of Sartre's theory

We are going to look at some of the foundations that underpin Sartre's theory. We have drawn these from his lecture, *Existentialism and Humanism*, and from *Being and Nothingness* and they should help us to see why he concludes that humans are absolutely free. The foundations depend upon phenomenology for their discovery and Sartre uses our experience of the world to support and illustrate these foundations. We think that there are four main foundations that support Sartre's theory:

1 Subjectivity and the *cogito*
2 Existence precedes essence

3 Atheism
4 Nothingness.

On pages 26–44 we explore these foundations, giving extracts from *E & H* that illustrate them. Just from reading some of the extracts it seems as if Sartre is identifying each foundation alone as the most important, the sole starting point of existentialism! This emphatic use of language is part of Sartre's style, but, as we analyse the foundations, we begin to notice their interdependence. The foundations are all interlinked, and we see them as essential building blocks for Sartre's existentialism.

Foundation 1: Subjectivity and the *cogito*

… we base our doctrine on pure subjectivity – upon the Cartesian 'I think'. (E & H, p. 23)

… we must begin from the subjective. (E & H, p. 26)

In *Existentialism and Humanism*, Sartre suggests that the starting point for existentialism is subjectivity, and the related idea of consciousness. We have therefore taken subjectivity as the first foundation of his theory. The concept of subjectivity is difficult enough to grasp in its normal sense, but Sartre, as we warned on page 9, uses it in his own special way.

ACTIVITY   **1** Write down as many sentences as you can which include the word 'subject' in them. Looking at these sentences, what are all the meanings of 'subject'? (Look in a dictionary if you want to.)
2 What is the difference between a 'subjective' and an 'objective' point of view?
3 How does the extract from *Nausea* that you read on pages 23–4 reveal Sartre's interest in the subjective?

There has been a long tradition in European philosophy, ever since Descartes (1596–1650), that philosophy should begin by examining the individual subject and what they are capable of knowing. This is in contrast to the view that philosophy can begin by looking at the things that surround us, the external world. Existentialists such as Kierkegaard and Sartre were a part of this tradition, believing that the individual comes first in philosophy, and Sartre in particular was impressed by Descartes' ideas about individual consciousness.

Descartes, in his books the *Meditations* and the *Discourse on Method*, tried to find something that he could be certain of and that he could not possibly doubt. He eventually discovered that he could not doubt that he was thinking, that he was conscious, and that he, Descartes, existed. He concluded: 'I think, therefore I am' or, as it is famously known in Latin, '*cogito ergo sum*'.[22] The phrase 'the *cogito*' refers to Descartes' philosophical discovery: the *cogito* means the act of recognising oneself as a necessarily conscious being. It was this idea of the *cogito* that Sartre found so important for his own philosophy; he refers to it as the truth upon which his theory is based.

And at the point of departure there cannot be any other truth than this, I think, therefore I am. (E & H, p. 44)

For Sartre, the *cogito* summed up our place in the universe: that we are not only conscious beings but also self-conscious, aware of our own thoughts and feelings.

Once Descartes had discovered the *cogito* as a point of certainty, he tried to move slowly from this to establish, with the same absolute certainty, the existence of the world around him. Most people agree that Descartes fails to do this. Sartre, though, is not really interested in trying to prove the existence of the world, he is simply trying to describe the world as it appears to a SELF-CONSCIOUS being. What Sartre and Descartes have in common is their belief that all genuine philosophical enquiry must begin with subjectivity.

Our point of departure is, indeed, the subjectivity of the individual. (E & H, p. 44)

This is an important idea for Sartre, and the quote gives us an insight into his philosophy. But there are some ambiguities about his claim, so let us look at these in detail.

Take the first phrase, 'point of departure'. Sartre could be claiming that the place where existentialism begins, its departure point, is with an analysis of individual subjectivity. On this account, 'point of departure' means the starting point of all existentialist enquiry (Figure 4.1).

■ **Figure 4.1**

subjectivity ▶ EXISTENTIALIST PHILOSOPHY ⟹

However, Sartre may also be making a further claim. For the existentialist, mainstream philosophy pretends to be neutral, objective and disengaged from the world. Sartre's phrase implies that subjectivity is the place at which existentialism departs from mainstream philosophy. And so, whilst the rest of philosophy blunders on with its foolish project to reach objective knowledge about the world, existentialism turns to focus on all that we can know: our own individual, subjective experiences (Figure 4.2).

■ **Figure 4.2**

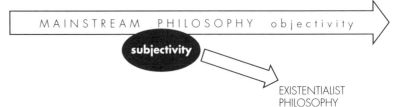

There is no other universe except the human universe, the universe of human subjectivity. (E & H, p. 55)

So, Sartre is rejecting objectivity and placing subjectivity at the heart of philosophy. This means that we can no longer pretend to be dispassionate observers of the world. We must admit our own personal engagement in the world, and our commitment to it. Existentialism demands that we act.

The second phrase, 'subjectivity of the individual', is also ambiguous, as Sartre himself recognises.

The word 'subjectivism' is to be understood in two senses . . . on the one hand, the freedom of the individual subject and, on the other, that man cannot pass beyond human subjectivity. (E & H, p. 29)

From this quotation we can see that Sartre gives his own special meaning to 'subjectivity', in the sense of 'the freedom of the individual subject'. We have already come across at least two ordinary meanings of 'subjective'. First, it could mean 'from a particular and individual point of view' (in contrast to 'objective', which means from an absolute and unbiased point of view). Second, subjectivity could mean the conscious and self-conscious experiences of an individual, which, for Sartre, is drawn from Descartes' idea of the *cogito*. These meanings of 'subjectivity' are connected, because they both refer to the subject, an individual (such as you) who is capable of having experiences. So, subjectivity could be the point of departure for Sartre's existentialism as follows:

■ Subjectivity is where existentialism departs from mainstream western philosophy because it explicitly rejects the possibility of objective knowledge.
■ Subjectivity means taking the experiences of the individual as the starting point for philosophical enquiry.

Both of these interpretations are connected with the phenomenological approach to philosophy outlined earlier on pages 21–5. Both interpretations also place the certainty of the *cogito* at the heart of existentialism: we must begin with our subjective experience of the world.

You need a blank piece of paper, a pen and a watch.

1 For two minutes write down as many of your feelings, thoughts, sensations, experiences as you can – everything you are aware of during those minutes.

2 Now (this is best done in pairs) group these experiences into categories, and keep trying to reduce these into fewer and fewer categories until you can go no further.

We have seen above how phenomenology begins with the experiences of the individual, rather than with abstract ideas or with the external world. In the Activity, by identifying, reflecting on and categorising your own experiences, you have started along the same philosophical route that a phenomenologist would take. Because Sartre takes a phenomenological approach, we find examples throughout *E & H* of raw and personal experiences. These he analyses in order to illustrate and support the ideas he puts forward.

Metaphysical interlude: Being-in-itself and being-for-itself

more difficult

■ The intentionality of consciousness

So how does Sartre, as a phenomenologist, analyse our experience of our subjectivity or consciousness? In the Activity, when you were writing down your experiences, were you ever conscious of nothing? Try to be conscious of nothing now . . . it's just not possible, at least not in the tradition of western philosophy and thought. In Sartre's view, all conscious experience is necessarily consciousness *of* or *about* something (this is an idea he borrowed from the German philosopher Husserl who himself had borrowed it from Brentano).[23] In other words, in order to think, we have to be thinking *about* something; we can never be conscious of nothing. In part 1 of the Activity you may have been thinking about money, or been angry at your friend, or been day-dreaming of chocolate chip ice-cream. All of these conscious states must have, or 'be aimed at', an object. This special quality of consciousness (its 'of-ness' or 'about-ness' or directedness) is known as its INTENTIONALITY (an idea used by Brentano and Husserl).

Look at the chair nearest to you. Think about it.

1 What materials is the chair made of?
2 Is the chair comfortable?
3 How long is the chair going to last before it is thrown away?

To help you to understand the intentionality of consciousness, you could try thinking of consciousness as a kind of ghostly arm, reaching out from your mind towards the world and grasping objects. So, for example, when you were thinking about how much longer the chair would last before it was thrown away, your consciousness was 'grabbing' the chair in order to consider the question (Figure 4.3):

■ **Figure 4.3**

Consciousness

The object of consciousness (a chair)

So, what kinds of things are we conscious of? Furniture, people, buildings, sights, sounds, smells, pickled cucumbers; the list goes on and on. In part 2 of the Activity on page 29 you may have found yourself grouping together all of your objects of consciousness into a very small number of categories:

■ experiences of things outside of yourself (for example, the sound of other people writing or of someone yawning)
■ experiences of things inside yourself (for example, your panic as you struggle to write something down, or the pains in your lower back).

■ Being-in-itself and being-for-itself

When Sartre considered the question of what kinds of things we are conscious of, he concluded that there were only two kinds: those that were objects, and those that were subjects, like us. This is his famous distinction between BEING-IN-ITSELF and BEING-FOR-ITSELF.

What is being-in-itself? The most obvious objects of consciousness are ordinary objects: tables, trees, roads, books, and so on. We are immediately aware of these objects as beings that are independent of our perceiving them; we cannot conjure them up whenever we please. According to Sartre, these objects are always initially perceived as outside of us: as independent existences that are resistant to our will. Sartre refers to such objects of experience as being-*in*-itself because they just are what they are, brute existents. Roquentin, in the extract from *Nausea* on pages 23–4, experienced the root of the tree as a being-in-itself. In *Being and Nothingness*, Sartre said that being-in-itself has no 'within'; in other words, no subjectivity. Being-in-itself is not conscious of anything, nor does it have any freedom and so it can never decide to change and become something else. A chair cannot suddenly decide to become a stool by shedding one of its legs, and a hedge cannot choose to grow into the shape of a poodle. We shall see later that being-in-itself has an essence and a pre-defined nature; material objects are tied to their past and do not possess any means to escape from it.

In contrast, we humans are being-*for*-itself. We saw on page 29 that consciousness is intentional; in other words, it is always aimed at some object. For much of the time, our awareness is directed on things outside of ourselves, for example, our mobile, the person sitting opposite us on the train, our dinner. However, our consciousness can also be directed back on itself, on to us. Figure 4.4 represents consciousness turning its attention to itself: self-consciousness. So, instead of the 'ghostly arm' (the direction and focus) of consciousness being aimed at something outside in the world (as in Figure 4.3), it is turned on itself (Figure 4.4).

■ **Figure 4.4**

Self-consciousness

1 Write down as many examples as you can of being self-conscious.
2 What feelings accompany self-consciousness? Are all of your examples of self-consciousness the same, or do some of them bring about different feelings?

There are lots of examples of your awareness directed inwards towards yourself: feeling guilty, feeling proud, feeling clumsy, looking in a mirror, feeling stared at, trying to remember what you were thinking a few moments ago, catching yourself picking your nose, wondering what you are going to do with your life. These are all examples of self-consciousness, of your consciousness directed on to itself.

So, being-for-itself is self-conscious, and Sartre believes that self-consciousness carries with it certain special qualities. We shall see later that Sartre identified self-consciousness (or being-for-itself) with 'nothingness'. This analysis of self-consciousness can be found in *B & N*, but for now we need only note some of the other qualities that arise from self-consciousness. Sartre says that self-consciousness means being able:

- to see ourselves as separate from the world
- to picture different possibilities for ourselves
- to imagine ourselves as different to who and what we are now
- to act without being acted upon, in other words, 'self-determination'.

▶ criticism ◀ We might ask where animals fit into Sartre's theory: are they in-itself or for-itself? His discussion of being-for-itself focuses solely on humans; whilst the examples he gives of being-in-itself tend to be artificial objects such as tables and knives. Sartre would probably have excluded animals from his conception of a 'conscious being'. But modern zoology suggests otherwise: many mammals behave in complex ways, they show signs of emotions, they may even have the capacity for language. Given what we know about animals, surely we would want to say that at least some of them were conscious? So why, then, does Sartre exclude them from his category of being-for-itself? It is very likely that Sartre, when he is talking about being-for-itself as conscious, is using 'consciousness' in a very particular way: he is linking it to subjectivity, to the possibility of the *cogito* and of self-consciousness.

The characteristics of the two aspects of being are as follows:

Being-for-itself	Being-in-itself
Conscious	Non-conscious
Open/unfinished	Closed/finished
Undetermined/free	Determined
Unpredictable	Predictable
Unrealised potential	Fully realised or 'actual'
No complete description possible	Complete description possible
Has no essence	Has an essence
Nothingness	Plenitude

The differences between being-for-itself and being-in-itself should begin to make more sense as we go through the other foundations of Sartre's theory below.

We have seen that the distinction between being-in-itself and being-for-itself arises from Sartre's analysis of subjectivity – of consciousness and the things we are aware of. This distinction is at the centre of Sartre's existentialism. Being-for-itself, those things that have the capacity of self-consciousness, take a central and special place in his philosophy. Most important, it is being-for-itself that turns out to be absolutely free, and it is the discovery of this freedom that makes Sartre's existentialism such an exciting philosophical theory.

So, the first foundation of Sartre's existentialism is subjectivity. For Sartre, this is the cornerstone not merely of all existentialist theories but of all philosophical theories. It implies a rejection of the traditional philosophical claim that we can describe, categorise or understand the world as if we were removed from it. Objectivity once provided an ivory tower from which many scientists and philosophers wanted to look down on the world and analyse it at a distance. But existentialists such as Sartre tore down this ivory tower and exposed philosophy to the reality of the world. For Sartre, philosophy begins with our personal encounter with the world, as self-conscious beings. Objectivity is impossible, and we must begin and end any philosophical investigation with subjectivity. Subjectivity means that we are bound by our own experiences of the world and, most important, we are bound to personal decisions and action in the world. Even as philosophers we must engage with the world, we must make choices, we must commit ourselves to action.

Foundation 2: Existence precedes essence

Sartre says in *E & H* that all existentialist philosophers are united in the belief that human beings do not have an essence, or that we exist before we have any essence.[24] We have identified this as the second foundation for Sartre's theory.

What they [existentialists] have in common is simply the fact that they believe that existence comes before essence. (E & H, p. 26)

What does Sartre mean when he says that existence comes before our essence? Sartre seems to answer this question himself later on in the lecture:

We mean that man first of all exists, encounters himself, surges up in the world – and defines himself afterwards . . . Man is nothing else but that which he makes of himself. That is the first principle of existentialism. (E & H, p. 28)

However, as with much of Sartre's lecture, these thoughts need careful interpretation.

In order to appreciate what lies behind the neat catchphrase 'existence precedes essence', we need to understand what the terms 'existence', 'precedes' and 'essence' mean. The twin concepts of existence and essence have a long philosophical history. The ideas go back to Aristotle. They were discussed by medieval philosophers, such as St Aquinas, who were influenced by Aristotle, and were concepts used centuries later by Descartes. For Descartes, as for his predecessors, reality could be viewed in two ways: what something is (what its defining features are) and whether something is (whether it exists). In answer to the question of *what* something is, a proper answer involves determining its essential nature. So, we could ask what a unicorn is, and try to give its defining characteristics, perhaps as a morally pure horse with a horn; this would be its *essence*. Of course, the *existence* of unicorns is a completely separate question, and would involve finding the lost City of Atlantis and searching for a horse with a horn by using a special net and a morally pure youth as bait.

Spending no more time than is necessary, give the essences (the defining characteristics) of the following objects:

Water   Pigeons   Dragons   Chairs   Pavements   Can-openers

Sartre's argument in *E & H* is that for humans, being-for-itself, our existence comes before any essence we might have. But for objects, being-in-itself, their essence comes first and it determines the kind of existence they will have. The example he gives to illustrate this point is of a paper-knife (a knife used to open envelopes or, in the past, sealed letters or the pages of books).

The paper-knife and human nature

ACTIVITY   Read pages 26–8 of *E & H* and think about the following questions:

1 In your own words, explain what Sartre means by 'essence'.
2 Where does the essence of the paper-knife come from?
3 Why does Sartre say that for the paper-knife its essence comes before its existence?
4 What would have to be the case if humans were to have an essence?
5 Does Sartre believe that humans have an essence?
6 Why/why not?
7 Is Sartre right?

The paper-knife has been designed for a particular purpose, and so it has an essence even before the artisan starts to make it. So, its essence comes before its existence. Its very existence depends upon the fact that someone has decided to create it for a particular purpose, and its future is mapped out in advance. This is important to Sartre, as it means that the paper-knife cannot change its essence, it cannot become anything different than what it is already. It cannot decide to be used as a throwing knife in a circus act, or as a murder weapon in an old mansion.

Sartre then considers what the world would have to be like if humans were to have an essence that preceded their existence. He argues there would have to be a 'SUPERNAL ARTISAN', in other words, a divine maker ('supernal' means divine or heavenly), who designed humans with a specific purpose in mind. Humans can have an essence only if there is a God to have given us one. If God had created us with a purpose in mind, before producing us, then, like the paper-knife, our essence would precede our existence. But Sartre argues that our existence precedes our essence.

His argument (E & H, p. 26) seems to go something like this:

- Premise 1 – If an object (for example, a paper-knife) has been designed then its essence precedes its existence.
- Premise 2 – For a human to have been designed there must have been a divine creator.
- Premise 3 – There is no divine creator.
- Premise 4 – Therefore humans have not been designed.
- Conclusion – Therefore, for humans, our existence precedes our essence, and so we are absolutely free.

So, if there is no God, and if man is not created by God, then humans have no intrinsic purpose. Humans just exist. For Sartre, it follows that existence is the primary fact about our condition with which we are faced, nothing else is true of us except that we exist. We do not have a purpose, we have not been designed for some specific task, and we do not have a predetermined future. This is what Sartre means by saying that existence precedes our essence. This implies that we are all free to create our own purpose or essence. But how are we to create a purpose for ourselves? Sartre's answer is through our actions. We create ourselves through what we choose to do. So, our essence, or what we are, is derived from what we do and the decisions we make. It is down to us to create ourselves, to make of ourselves what we are.

By saying that 'existence precedes essence', Sartre is once again distinguishing existentialism from the mainstream of philosophy. In contrast to Sartre, most other philosophers believe that there is a human nature. We could characterise those who believe that our essence precedes our existence as 'essentialists'; this is in contrast to the 'existentialists' who believe that our existence comes first.

Sartre was disappointed by secular philosophers who believed that there is a certain nature which is common to all men and fixed for all time. This view of human beings requires that 'the wild man of the woods ... and the bourgeois are ... contained in the same definition and have the same fundamental qualities' (*E & H*, p. 27). Such a view, according to Sartre, simply reinstates the religious attitude that the essence of man precedes his existence. Many philosophers have talked about human nature. For example, Aristotle sees us as essentially political animals; Plato as essentially rational; Hobbes as selfish; and some humanists as essentially good. Similarly, scientists claim that we have a biological nature which determines what we are as human beings. All such views suggest we are defined by our essence. But Sartre sees us as essentially *nothing*. For him, every philosopher prior to existentialism was missing the point. We have no essence, we have nothing at our core, we are bound to nothing, fixed by nothing, determined by nothing.

There is no human nature, according to Sartre, which can give us an essence. Neither is there any fixed personality, or inner self or soul, which can give us an essence. Any attempt to fix someone's character or personality by labelling them as 'cowardly' or 'criminal' is to deny the truth about their being, namely their lack of essence. No name-calling or assignment of roles can determine what we may become; no description of our past lives captures what we could be in the future. The description 'coward' necessarily comes after the fact and individuals can always redefine themselves by changing their actions. Unlike being-in-itself, humans are essentially indefinable.

Sartre, to illustrate his point that we have no essence, gives the example of the French novelist Marcel Proust, a writer considered by many to be a genius because of the psychological and emotional depth of his novels.[25] But this genius was not something with which he was born, or which preceded his novels. According to Sartre, Proust did not possess any essential genius which was the cause of his great works. Instead, Sartre says, Proust's genius *is* his works, or his genius is constituted through his works (*E & H*, pp. 41–2). If Proust had died and had written only sketchy ideas on the backs of envelopes, and had not got round to writing his novels, then he would not have been a genius. This goes for all of us, we create ourselves (our essence, if you like) through what we do. As Sartre says:

> *Man is . . . nothing else but the sum of his actions.*
> (E & H, *p. 41*)

Evaluation of Sartre's claim that our existence precedes our essence

▶ criticism ◀   If we have no essence, then why does Sartre say that our existence *precedes* our essence? This implies that, although we may exist first, at some point we acquire an essence. But Sartre says that we have no essence. He seems to be contradicting himself by asserting, on the one hand, that we have no essence whilst, on the other, suggesting that we do get an essence after we exist.

⚠️
more difficult

Stephen Priest offers a solution to this problem when he suggests that 'precedes' can be interpreted either chronologically or logically.[26] To precede something chronologically is to come before it in time, for example, our youth precedes our old age. If Sartre is thinking of 'precedes' in this sense, then he may be thinking of our essence as something we acquire when we die. When we die we do have an essence: we are the sum of all the things we did in life and can do nothing more to change this. So, 'existence precedes essence' may mean that we exist first, but eventually we die and can make no more choices, hence we get an essence. What is so depressing about Sartre's play *No Exit* (in French *Huis Clos*) is that the three characters, who have all died and gone to hell, begin to realise that they can do nothing to change themselves or the type of people they are: they are dead and now have a permanent essence.[27]

Sartre may also be thinking of 'precedes' in the logical sense, meaning 'to be a requirement or precondition' of something. For example, a triangle could not be a triangle without having straight sides, so 'having straight sides' *precedes*, or is a precondition of, a shape being a triangle. If Sartre is using 'precedes' in this sense, then he means that our existence is a necessary precondition for our essence. In other words, we cannot be defined in advance, unlike a knife or a table or some other functional object. We cannot say that, just because someone comes from a family of corrupt politicians, they too are going to be a corrupt politician. We have no predefined essence, but instead each of us must first of all exist, and then, as Sartre says, define ourselves afterwards (*E & H*, p. 28).

▶ criticism ◀ Is it really true that humans do not have an essence? We might object that surely it is obvious that someone like Proust must have had some special characteristics which enabled him to write the works he did, such as his insight, his industry, his intelligence. Moreover, even if we are not created by God, we none the less have genes and childhoods which make us the people we are. We cannot simply choose to be whoever we want to be! This is an important objection to Sartre and one to which we will need to return.

▶ criticism ◀ Do other living things have an essence or not? Sartre states (*E & H*, p. 28) that moss, fungus and cauliflower are objects that possess no 'subjective life', in other words, their essence precedes their existence. If this is true, then this seems to imply that they have been designed. But surely Sartre would also wish to deny that the natural world has been designed, otherwise he is on his way to admitting that there is a divine creator? This problem arises for Sartre because he equates 'essence' with 'design' in his example of the paper-knife. We can avoid the problem by saying that 'essence' implies possessing any sort of determining feature, natural or non-natural. On this account we can claim that plants have an essence, and are determined by their physical make-up, but do not have to accept the existence of God. But the criticism remains that Sartre is vague as to what he means by essence, and he says little in the lecture to clarify this concept.[28]

One response to this would be to say that living things do not have any real essence. This may be the point that Roquentin (in the extract from *Nausea* on pages 23–4) is exploring when he sees that seagulls and roots in themselves are just brute existents. Any essence they may be thought to have is one imposed on them by us, in part through language (hence Roquentin's talk about their losing their names and with that their meaning/essence). But all that this means is that the essences of things depend upon us. We create them literally, in our factories and workshops, and metaphorically, in the words we use to talk about the world.

This solution may lead to a further problem.

▶ criticism ◀ If we can make sense of the idea that things can have essences without being created, then the argument that we *cannot* have an essence because there is no God fails. This is because there need not be a creator in order for something to have an essence. An argument along these lines may be one that a scientist or geneticist might want to pursue. For example, Charles Darwin might say that there can be design (in the sense that the parts work together for a purpose) without a designer (a billion years of evolution has the effect of 'design'). But Sartre has independent phenomenological reasons for thinking that we do not have an essence, namely the lived experience of our freedom. We shall come back to this in the section on 'Nothingness' (page 42).

Further problems arise when we try to pin down what Sartre means by our essence.

► criticism ◄ Sometimes in the lecture Sartre talks as if humans do have an essence. For example, he says that we are all free, or that there is a 'universality to the human condition', something that we all share. At other times he denies that we have an essence because we are absolutely free. Could our essence be our freedom? Or our lack of essence? A further difficulty here is that Sartre's talk of our creating our essence through our actions is paradoxical. We do not really create an essence, since it is constantly open to revision. It may be due to the brevity of the lecture, or to his assumption that we all understand what essence means, but Sartre fails to explain what he does mean by 'essence', and hence leaves his ideas open to these kind of problems.

When we look at *Being and Nothingness* for guidance, Sartre's position seems clearer. At one point Sartre says that 'my essence is what I have been' (*B & N*, p. 450). In other words, my essence is my past, and all the things that I have done to contribute to my past.[29] So, my present existence, and the actions I take now, add to my essence like the shell of a snail which it carries around and which gets larger and larger. My essence, then, can be seen as 'the things that would define me if were I to die today'.

Foundation 3: Atheism

Closely related to the idea that existence precedes essence is the third foundation we have identified in *Existentialism and Humanism*: that God does not exist.

Dostoyevsky once wrote 'If God did not exist, everything would be permitted'; and that, for existentialism, is the starting point. (E & H, p. 33)

We have already encountered Sartre's atheism in two guises. First, we have seen on page 35 Sartre's proposition that a divine artisan has not designed humans and that therefore human existence precedes essence and so we are absolutely free. Second, we have seen in the extract from *Nausea* on pages 23–4 how the main character suddenly realises that everything in the world is 'superfluous'. Roquentin begins to believe that if there is no God then there is no meaning or purpose to anything in the universe.

There is a further, more important aspect to Sartre's atheism, which forms the main focus of *E & H*. It is revealed in the quotation on page 39 from *E & H*. In Dostoyevsky's book *The Brothers Karamazov*, one of the characters, Ivan Karamazov, argues that if there is no God to create moral laws or to judge our souls after we die, then effectively we are free to do anything we choose: 'everything would be permitted, even cannibalism'.[30] Philosophers have often drawn a close connection between God and morality, and Sartre considers it impossible to believe that there are any *A PRIORI* moral values without a divine underpinning. If there is a God, then it would be possible to know *a priori*, prior to and independent of our own experiences, the objective moral rules that He has laid down for us to follow. If there is no God, then what we are left with, as Sartre says, is 'extremely embarrassing' (*E & H*, p. 33): namely, the disappearance of objective morality altogether. This is a shocking thought, and one that Sartre acknowledges right at the beginning of *E & H*:

For since we ignore the commandments of God and all values prescribed as eternal, nothing remains but what is strictly voluntary. Everyone can do what he likes.
(E & H, p. 24)

experimenting with ideas

The next time you leave your front door, try looking around you to find out what everything means. What are all these people doing, who are running around? If there is no God, what is the point?

In later chapters we shall examine how humans react to this 'abandonment' by God; we shall assess the criticism that existentialism permits every action, however horrific; and we shall see how Sartre attempts to construct an existential morality which does not depend on God.

As with the other foundations, problems arise from Sartre's atheism.

▶ criticism ◀ In *E & H*, Sartre simply assumes that God does not exist. But both believers and agnostics (who are undecided about God's existence) would disagree with Sartre's assumption. They would want Sartre to demonstrate that atheism is a more reliable or justifiable foundation than that of faith in God. Without such a demonstration of the strength of atheism against its alternatives, they might reject the rest of Sartre's theory. However, Sartre is concerned only with taking his atheist assumption to its full conclusion, and he is not interested in proving or disproving the existence of God.

In Sartre's main existentialist work, *B & N*, our status as being-for-itself, and hence as being free, is established independently of whether or not there is a God.[31] In *E & H*, it is possible that Sartre used the idea of the divine artisan only in order to get across the idea of our freedom quickly and clearly to his audience, so that he could move on to the main concern of his lecture: a defence of his theory.

► criticism ◄ As Sartre admits, there are many Christian existentialists.[32] For example, Kierkegaard was a devout believer and is considered to be the father of existentialism. This once again shows the weakness of Sartre's paper-knife example (*E & H*, p. 26), because Christian existentialists believe in God as a divine artisan, but they also believe that humans are absolutely free.

What we can say is that God's existence may be irrelevant to our subjective experience of the world. Some believers, such as Kierkegaard, took a leap of faith towards believing in a Christian God without having had any experience of God and without knowing what God's purpose was for them. These existentialist believers may feel just as abandoned and just as free as do existentialist atheists, such as Sartre. Even if God has designed us with a particular purpose in mind, and we discover what it is, it is still up to us whether we fulfil this purpose. The key to existentialism lies not in atheism but in our experience of ourselves as free, self-conscious beings.

At the end of *E & H* (p. 56), Sartre more or less admits that atheism is irrelevant to the project of existentialism. He says that existentialists are not concerned with disproving the existence of God, and that God's existence or non-existence makes no difference to his argument. Some might say that Sartre's existentialism requires him to be an agnostic (someone who remains undecided) rather than an atheist.

Sartre's main foundations for existentialism and his belief in the absolute freedom of humans are not based on atheism or our lack of essence. The main foundations are phenomenological ones, based on the analysis of self-consciousness, which we have looked at already, and of nothingness, to which we shall turn next.

Foundation 4: Nothingness

more difficult

In *B &N*, Sartre employs phenomenology to analyse consciousness or being-for-itself. He discovers something peculiar: that at the core of our being is nothingness – a gap, a space, a negation. This nothingness, for Sartre, is the key to our freedom. Sartre does not really refer to nothingness in *E & H*, and it is not essential to understand it in order to understand his lecture. But he does talk of humans as 'nothing' and as 'TRANSCENDENT' or 'SELF-SURPASSING'. If we want to have a better grasp of Sartre's existentialism, then it is worth examining this strange and difficult idea.

If man as the existentialist sees him is not definable, it is because to begin with he is nothing. (E & H, p. 28)

What is nothingness? Sartre seems to mean many things by nothingness, and we give some examples below. One way of beginning to understand what Sartre means by nothingness is to go back to his analysis of consciousness. Remember, as discussed on page 29, that Sartre claimed that consciousness is always consciousness *of* something. This means that consciousness itself cannot be an object for itself. In other words, when we think about ourselves we are never aware of 'consciousness' but always of some particular experience or sensation. So, strictly speaking, we cannot be conscious of our 'self'. We could think of consciousness as a kind of container – it 'holds' our experiences, but is in itself nothing since we cannot experience it. Sartre sometimes expresses this idea by saying that the self, or consciousness, is a kind of gap in being or 'nothingness'.

When Sartre talks about nothingness, he is also trying to describe a special feature of our experience of the world. Humans (being-for-itself) have the capacity consciously to detach themselves from the world. We can imagine things that have not yet happened, we can create things that do not yet exist, we can decide to change our usual habits, we can question the way things are. All of these capacities, for Sartre, indicate a power to 'negate' the world – to see it as different and distinct from us. And, Sartre says, we have this power because we ourselves are nothingness.

Sartre gives many descriptions of negation in *B & N*. Below are a few of the examples that he gives of our experience of nothingness, examples which, for Sartre, show that at the core of our being is nothingness:

■ He describes how he arrives late for a meeting with a friend in a café. He looks around and considers each face in turn

then negates it as 'not the face of my friend' and so each
face, as it is negated in his consciousness, merges once
again into the background.[33]

- In his autobiography *Words*, Sartre describes how, when he
  was young, he went to a party with his grandfather. During
  the evening his grandfather realised someone was missing
  from the party: his best friend Simonnot. Sartre is struck by
  his experience of Simonnot's absence: it is a concrete
  absence, an emptiness in the room, a kind of nothingness.[34]
- In *B & N*, Sartre finds negation in our capacity to reject
  (or 'negate') our past and to change our habits. For
  example, someone who is addicted to gambling can resolve
  no longer to play cards. The mere fact that they once
  gambled every day does not determine their future actions.
  For Sartre, we are not chained to any fixed personality or
  disposition or essence.[35]
- In *B & N*, Sartre describes the feeling of vertigo we get
  when we are walking along a precipice without any railing
  to hold on to. This feeling of vertigo arises because of the
  capacity we have to imagine all the horrific ways in which
  we could fall and die. But we can 'negate' each of these
  futures. In other words, we can say to ourselves, 'I am not
  that future.' Being able to imagine these different possible
  futures leads us to act carefully to avoid all such possible
  ways of dying.[36]

So, one of the most important aspects of nothingness is that
we can negate our past and imagine all our future possibilities.
This is what Sartre refers to in *E & H* when he says that
humans are 'self-surpassing' (p. 55). Sartre might say that
there is a 'gap' between our present and our past and so we
can transcend it: what we have done before does not
determine what we are capable of doing now. There is also a
gap between where we are now and our future. Our lives are
not on tram rails, with fate pulling us or scientific
determinism pushing us in one direction into the future.
Instead, we are able to imagine lots of different futures, to
'project' ourselves into the future, and to choose between
different goals. Figure 4.5 (overleaf) illustrates the gaps
between our present and our past and future.[37]

In contrast to this, objects, or being-in-itself, are
completely determined by their past and their future is a
given. Their essence makes them what they are and means
that they can never be any different. So, a chair is a chair is a
chair. Figure 4.6 (overleaf) attempts to illustrate this point.

Despite the striking examples that Sartre uses to illustrate
his concept of nothingness, it still strikes people as a deeply
puzzling idea.

■ **Figure 4.5**

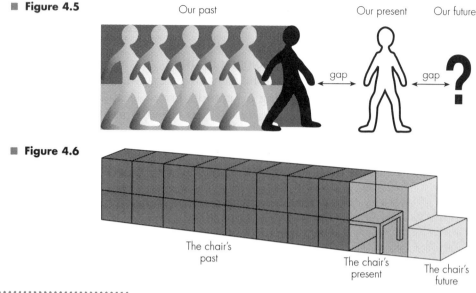

Our past   Our present   Our future

gap   gap

?

■ **Figure 4.6**

The chair's
past

The chair's
present

The chair's
future

▶ criticism ◀ Many philosophers have rejected Sartre's idea as incoherent.
Does it really make sense to talk about nothingness in the
ways that Sartre does? He believes that he is describing some
positive feature of our experience of the world, and it is true
that the examples he describes are ones we can all vividly
imagine, but how are they all connected? The examples do
not appear to have much in common, except perhaps that
they are all about one thing *not* being something else.

Surely, one might argue, we should not talk about
nothingness as though it were a strange kind of thing
contrasted with being? It is simply the absence of any being.
Rather than thinking of the word 'nothingness' as designating
some integral aspect of our experience and giving it a deep
philosophical significance, perhaps we should see it as a word
used to help us to talk of things that are not there. If you
have found Sartre's concept of nothingness particularly
perplexing, you are in good company as many philosophers
have difficulty explaining his idea. It may just be that Sartre is
no longer making good sense!

In this chapter we have looked at Sartre's philosophical
method and have picked out four concepts that we think
provide the foundations of Sartre's existentialism. In the
coming chapters we shall look at the implications that these
foundations have for our lives, as described in Sartre's theory.
What follows from these foundations goes to the very core of
our being (METAPHYSICAL implications – Chapter 5); it affects
our feelings and attitudes to the world (emotional
implications – Chapter 6); and it affects our understanding of
how we should live (ethical implications – Chapters 7 and 8).

Key points: Chapter 4

What you need to know about the **foundations** of Sartre's existentialism:

1 Sartre relied on phenomenology as his method of doing philosophy. This meant that he began his philosophy with an analysis of his experiences of the world.

2 We suggest that there are four foundations underpinning Sartre's theory. Some of these can be found in *E & H* and others in *B & N*. We believe that, in order to understand *E & H* fully, you need to know something about all four foundations.

3 The first foundation we identify is subjectivity. This means that philosophy must begin (as Descartes showed with his *cogito*) with our own consciousness and our own experiences. Any attempt at objectivity is a mistake.

4 Sartre's own analysis of subjectivity in *B & N* led him to the conclusion that there are two types of being in the world: being-in-itself (i.e. material objects) and being-for-itself (i.e. self-conscious beings like ourselves). Being-for-itself is special because we are able to determine what and who we are.

5 The second foundation is 'existence precedes essence'. Material objects have an essence, or a physical nature, which determines exactly what they are and what they will be. Humans, on the other hand, do not have an essence or nature. This is because there is no God who has made us with an essence in mind. Without an essence we exist first, and we invent ourselves as we go along.

6 The third foundation is atheism. Like many philosophers, Sartre assumes that there is no God. However, unlike some atheists, Sartre is prepared to draw the conclusions of atheism to the very end. This means realising that there is no objective basis for morality. It also means acknowledging that humans have no essence, and that we have no given purpose in our lives.

7 The fourth foundation we have identified is nothingness. This comes from Sartre's earlier book, *B & N*, and is not mentioned in *E & H*. But, for Sartre, it is the most important part of our freedom. Nothingness is the gap between us (as self-conscious beings) and the world; between us and our past; between us and our future. Because there is this leeway, we are free to choose our own future and to reject our past.

5
Metaphysical implications: Freedom and facticity

Introduction

Read *E & H* pages 28–9, 34 and 42–4

In this chapter we are going to be looking at some of the metaphysical consequences of the foundations Sartre has laid. The consequences are 'metaphysical' because of their implications for who we *really* are and for what our relation *really* is to the external world. What implications for our lives and our actions does Sartre's theory have? What follows if it is true that objectivity is impossible, or that we have no essence, or that there is no God? The chapter is divided as follows:

- Sartre's concept of freedom
- Facticity
- Evaluation of Sartre's claim that we are free
- Key points you need to know about the metaphysical implications of the foundations.

Sartre's concept of freedom

The most significant impact of Sartre's theory on our lives is his conclusion that we are absolutely free. But what enables Sartre to draw such a dramatic conclusion? Depending on whether we read *B & N* or *E & H*, our freedom stems respectively from our nothingness or from our lack of an essence. In *B & N*, Sartre begins from an analysis of subjectivity, placing philosophy firmly in the individual and their experiences of the world. Some of the defining experiences that we, as humans, are capable of having reveal the nothingness at the core of our being. We are detached from the world of material objects; we have the capacity to escape our past, to imagine our possible futures and so we are able to choose our actions freely. This is the route to freedom that Sartre takes in *B & N* (Figure 5.1).

From another angle, in *E & H*, Sartre defines our subjectivity in terms of our lack of essence. God does not exist and we must 'draw the consequences of his absence right to the end' (*E & H*, p. 33). Because there is no God to have designed us, we have no essence. We exist first and we invent and reinvent ourselves throughout our lives. This route also takes us to the conclusion that we are free (Figure 5.1).

■ **Figure 5.1**

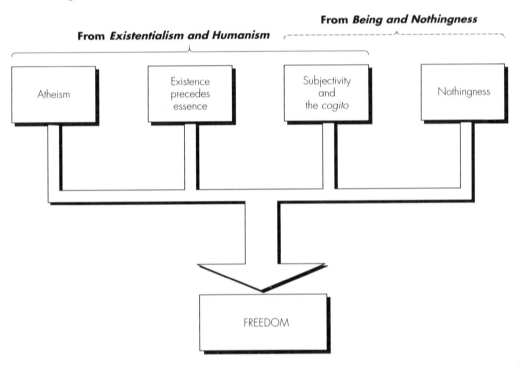

So Sartre, if he is right, has shown that humans are free because we are neither being pushed by the past nor pulled towards the future. We are not pushed, because our actions are not caused by our past. Our biology, our genetic make-up, our upbringing, our schooling is all in the past but, because of the gap between us and our past, we are free to choose our attitude to it: to embrace it or reject it as we wish. Nor are we pulled because there is no set path, no fate or destiny laid down for us in advance. We were not placed on Earth for any purpose, we do not have to seek one or follow one. Nor are there are any moral rules that we are obliged to follow. So, humans are absolutely, one hundred per cent, free.

For if indeed existence precedes essence, one will never be able to explain one's action by reference to a given and specific human nature; in other words, there is no determinism – man is free, man is freedom. (E & H, p. 34)

'Freedom' can mean many things and we should distinguish between two of its important senses: METAPHYSICAL FREEDOM and political freedom. Political freedom means both being able to participate in the political processes of our country and remaining free from political oppression. Political freedom is purely a social phenomenon, it varies from society to society, and it includes things such as freedom of speech, freedom to vote or freedom of assembly. On the other hand, metaphysical freedom (or freedom of the will, or free will) refers to the freedom we have, as individuals, to make choices and to act on these choices. It is not a social phenomenon, but is part of our make-up as being-for-itself, and so does not vary amongst individuals. Sartre placed a high value on both types of freedom, but his existentialist theory is concerned mainly with metaphysical freedom.

Metaphysical freedom implies that if we are faced with only two possible choices, A and B, then the decision to choose B and not A is ours alone. Moreover, if we turned back the clock and faced the same two choices, then we could make a completely different decision. Our freedom is absolute, we have total control over our actions, there is nothing outside of ourselves that caused it, and the source of the action lies solely in us.

Unlike political freedom, metaphysical freedom is a fact not a value.[38] Political freedom is something that people fight for if they do not have it, and something that they think should be protected and preserved if they do have it. Metaphysical freedom, on the other hand, is not something to be fought for or preserved in law: it is not an optional part of our lives, but is a part of our very condition. Metaphysical freedom is what we are and there is nothing we can do about it. A prisoner who is locked in chains, and who has lost all his political freedom, would still be as metaphysically free as the richest millionaire in Beverley Hills. This is because the prisoner is still absolutely free to choose to take up an attitude to his imprisonment.[39] He can give in to his jailers or he can resist them with his thoughts and words.[40]

Sartre's conception of freedom is a very empowering one and was developed by Simone de Beauvoir to potent effect in her influential book, *The Second Sex*. This was a book written to show how women are oppressed by men and how they accept this oppression because they do not realise the basic fact of the human condition: that there is no human nature.[41] De Beauvoir urges women to recognise their freedom and to transcend the oppressive social roles that men have given them.

However, although Sartre's claim that we are absolutely free is a thrilling one, there are problems with it. From without, it is threatened by the competing philosophical theory of determinism; from within, it is threatened by our denial and refusal to acknowledge our freedom.

Freedom and determinism

There are many thinkers who do not agree that we have free will. Many will argue in favour of determinism, in other words that all our thoughts and actions are pre-determined.

Read the comments of six critics of Sartre (below) and for each of them answer the following questions:

a) What kind of criticism are they making of Sartre's theory?

b) How do you think Sartre might respond to their comments?

Critic 1 'Sartre, I don't mean to patronise, but you know that we live in a physical world, governed by physical laws, right? Now, surely you don't believe we have a soul – we just have a brain, right? Agreed. Well, our brain is a physical organ and so our thoughts and actions are governed by the same physical laws as everything else. So, our actions are as determined as a rock falling from the Grand Canyon on to a racoon.'

Critic 2 'Comrade Sartre, the history of humanity is governed by certain rules, unavoidable patterns that are doomed to be repeated, despite the efforts of the individual. Your so-called individual freedom is irrelevant compared to vast social and economic forces at work beneath the surface. I urge you to give up on this bourgeois folly and to join the revolution – it will be a bloodless one this time.'

Critic 3 'Monsieur Sartre, you yourself acknowledged, in your revealing autobiography *Words*, that certain events in your childhood changed your life forever. I am referring, of course, to the death of your father when you were only a few months old. You would surely agree that a baby has no freedom, but is subject to the whims and wishes of its carers. The socialisation and experiences of children, from an early age, determine the habits of a lifetime. By the time we are old enough to even think about the philosophical question of free will it is all too late. Our thoughts and behaviour patterns have already been set and our freedom is a fairy tale. If you would like to make an appointment to see me, I charge forty francs per hour.'

Critic 4 'Hey, Jean-Paul! I don't know much about philosophy, but I do know that my experience of the world isn't always too accurate. On a hot day, man, I get to see pools of water in the road, but they don't quench my thirst, they're just a trick of light in the heat. And when I had jaundice everything I saw was yellow, but I knew I was mistaken. I'm sure the mescaline didn't help, but you should know all about that. So, although you're right, I sure do feel free, mighty free, how do I know that this feeling isn't just another illusion, just another trick of my mind?'

Critic 6 'Sartre, I don't know what the hell you're going on about. It's like you philosophers are living in the Stone Age or something. Freedom? You must be kidding! Now, you may have heard about a little thing called DNA – genetics, if you like. Well, my laboratory is well on its may to discovering the programming of each and everyone of us. In the next twenty years we'll be able to tell, just from a drop of a baby's blood, exactly what kind of person it's going to be. Now, I suggest to you that you drop all this dangerous, medieval claptrap and go study a bit of science. Thank you, I've said my piece.'

Critic 5 'Monsieur Professeur, although you dismissed my comments about the smile of an infant in a most distressing and humiliating manner, I do forgive you. Please could you explain once again just how exactly we have free will, given that there is an almighty, all-knowing creator of this world?'

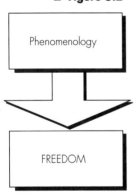

The examples in the activity suggest that there are philosophers and scientists queuing up to disparage Sartre's theory of absolute freedom. And it does seem hard to deny that our bodies, including our brains, are subject to, and determined, by the physical laws of the universe. Determinists argue that we do not have free will because all of our actions are necessitated, or causally determined, by what came before. In other words, we could not have acted in any other way except the way we did act. 'Pick a card, any card,' says the street magician, so we choose one. Now imagine turning back time and being asked the same question. For the determinist, we would choose exactly the same card. If the determinist is correct, then Sartre's theory of freedom is under serious threat.

The traditional way of side-stepping the 'free will or determinism' dilemma is to take the view that they are compatible and not contradictory ideas. The so-called 'compatibilist' accepts that our actions are caused, but argues that a free act is one where the cause is internal to us (see page 66 and note 59). For example, we feel like having an ice-cold drink on a blistering summer day, so we choose to buy one. For the compatibilist, the real threat to freedom comes from people forcing us to do something, for example, to drink scalding soup on a hot day at gunpoint.

■ Figure 5.2

Phenomenology

FREEDOM

But Sartre does not need to take a compatibilist position to avoid the problems of determinism.[42] His theory of freedom may be immune to determinism, because he is concerned only with what we may call 'phenomenological freedom'. This is our inner experience of freedom, and of being confronted by it every day of our lives. For Sartre, we do not actually ever experience determinism by introspection, it is merely a 'faith to take refuge in'.[43] On the other hand, we encounter choice all the time, and it is this experience of freedom, and our response to this experience, in which Sartre is really interested. So, we have further reason for concluding that we are free: our phenomenological experience of freedom (Figure 5.2).

Our rejection of freedom

Write down three actions (within your physical capacities) that you would take NOW, if you were absolutely free.

There are many reasons why we do not do all of the things that we could choose to do. But Sartre's point is that these are real possibilities for us, so why do we not do them? What is stopping us?

- In the case of the activity on page 50, it may be that we have chosen to ignore the given instruction and that what we would like to do is a physical impossibility for humans, such as flying without wings. We shall deal with these limits to our absolute freedom in the section on facticity (see page 53).
- Freedom brings overwhelming responsibility; at times we must carry the weight of the world on our shoulders,[44] and this is something that most people want to avoid at all costs. If choice is an unavoidable consequence of freedom, then responsibility is an unavoidable consequence of choice. If we are free then the buck stops with us: we are the sole cause of our actions and we must bear responsibility for them. Accepting responsibility for all that we do is a frightening idea, and we would much rather pretend that we were not free, or that we were not responsible. We shall look at the anguish that responsibility brings when we consider the emotional implications of existentialism in Chapter 6.

The first effect of existentialism is that it puts every man in possession of himself as he is, and places the entire responsibility for his existence squarely upon his own shoulders. (E & H, p. 29)

- We do not consider all possible choices to be 'live possibilities'.[45] In other words, there are some things which we are physically able to do but which we just would never consider doing, because they do not contribute to the goals that we have at the time. For example, we could stop whatever we are doing now and start hitchhiking across Europe. But this would entail giving up many of the projects that we have established in order to reach our chosen aims (such as our job or education, our friendships or love). Hitchhiking across Europe is not, then, a live possibility. But Sartre would say that we choose our goals, and thus we can make something a live possibility by reconsidering what we want to achieve in life.[46]
- Freedom is exhausting.[47] According to Sartre, we are actually condemned to be free (*E & H*, p. 34) and to reinvent ourselves continually. In other words, we did not choose to be born free, we did not tick that particular box in the womb, and we cannot escape being free whilst we live. Such unavoidable freedom is a drag. To wake up and reinvent ourselves day after day takes so much effort that it's much better to stick with our old routines: brush teeth and hair, put cat in garden, forget keys as front door slams shut.

In the following scenarios people perform different actions.

a) Think about whether the act that the person performs is free. (Consider whether the person should be held responsible for it.)

b) Do you think that Sartre would agree with you? What would you say to defend your answer if he disagreed?

---

1 It is Valentine's Day and Ross wants to do something special to commemorate it for his wife Amelia. On his way home, Ross pops into the video store and gets the latest romantic comedy – the one his wife had especially asked for at Christmas, but which he had forgotten to buy. (*Did Ross freely choose that video?*)

---

3 Tim is a man of strong principles. He believes that it is always wrong to kill animals for food. One day he is shipwrecked on a desert island and finds that the only nourishment available to sustain life is the flesh of small rodents. True to his principles, he chooses not to kill and dies an agonising death from starvation. (*Is Tim's choice to die a free one?*)

---

5 All her life, Emma is told that her role in life will be to get married and be a good wife and mother. When she is sixteen, her father finds an eligible bachelor and tells her that she should accept his offer of marriage. The bachelor is very rich, but somewhat portly and decidedly ugly, with bad breath. Emma agrees to the marriage and settles into a life of drudgery. (*Does Emma freely agree to marriage?*)

---

7 Shaz comes from a rich family. She is young and beautiful but rather naïve. One day, she meets Luke and falls passionately in love with him. Unfortunately, Luke is a nasty piece of work and sees an opportunity to make some money. Luke convinces Shaz to marry him and to kill her father so that they can inherit his fortune. Shaz is afraid to lose Luke and so agrees. (*Does Shaz freely choose to kill her father?*)

---

2 Charlie sleepwalks to the fridge late one night and drinks a pint of skimmed milk, which he would not normally touch as he is a big fan of full fat milk. (*Did Charlie freely drink the milk?*)

---

4 Andrew has a terrible fear of snakes. Whenever he even thinks of one he goes into cold sweats and does crazy things. One fine morning, while holidaying with his family in the tropics, he wanders into his sister's bedroom to call her for breakfast. Suddenly he spies a boa constrictor in the corner of the room. Overcome by fear he flees from the room in panic and bars the door, locking in his sister with the snake. His sister is swallowed by the snake. (*Is the act of barring the door free?*)

---

6 Jack has noticed an interesting fact about his school career. Whenever he is set a piece of homework, he forgets all about it until the lesson when he is supposed to submit it. He concludes from this that he must have a terrible memory. One day, Jack is given a piece of very important work to do. He decides to make a special effort, but unfortunately finds himself back in class without having done it. (*Did Jack freely choose not to do his homework?*)

---

8 Ben is thinking of murdering Madeleine but, being a sporting kind of guy, he decides not to make it too easy and to give her a fighting chance. He prepares a cup of coffee and a cup of tea and puts arsenic in the tea. Then he asks Madeleine if she would like a cup of tea or coffee. Madeleine chooses tea and dies. (*Does Madeleine freely choose to die?*)

- Finally, we find freedom terrifying, and we stop like a rabbit in headlights when we have to face up to all the live possibilities it brings. There are only a few occasions in our life when freedom really slaps us in the face. One such occasion might be leaving college with no job to go to, without the safety net of 'term-times' and 'lessons' to arrange our lives around. Perhaps losing a loved one, ending a relationship, or being made redundant from a job are other times when we are confronted by our freedom. These are all circumstances when the neat structure to our lives suddenly disappears, and we are faced with something that we pretended we did not have: freedom. The fear we have of our freedom leads to our denial of it, and this 'bad faith' is something we shall focus on in Chapter 7.

Freedom is the crux of Sartre's existentialism; it distinguishes it from all other philosophies. Freedom is conveyed as invigorating and powerful by Sartre, but also as fearful. We experience it initially through our anguish, but then it hits us like a kind of eruption of consciousness – we are suddenly able to break through our anguish and we act. Sartre urges us to embrace freedom; to take decisions, make choices, and implement projects in order to give human existence some meaning. Indeed, from a Sartrean perspective, our whole life becomes a kind of project: we choose who we want to be and continually go about creating ourselves. We are free to choose *any* action and *any* goal and to invent our lives, to 'draw our own portrait' (*E & H*, p. 42). But there are limits to our freedom.

Facticity

When we first read of Sartre's assertion that we are absolutely free, we immediately think, 'no, we're not,' and list some of the things that we would like to do but cannot: we are not free to fly to the moon and play amongst the stars; we are not free to win the lottery. Sartre seems to be obviously wrong. However, if we think in this way, we are confusing freedom with omnipotence (being all-powerful); these are two very different concepts. To say that we have absolute freedom is not to say that we have the power to do anything and everything. Freedom has limits, which is why it differs from omnipotence.[48]

ACTIVITY   **1** What are the limits of your own freedom? What facts about you are beyond your control?

2 Read page 46 of *E & H*. What are the limitations on the human condition that Sartre identifies here?

Sartre is no idealistic fool. He does not think that our physical circumstances, our economic situation or our past actions make no difference at all to our freedom. Sartre acknowledges the limits of freedom to be all those facts that are true of us but that we cannot choose to change.

Some general things that we are not free to choose include: our place of birth, our parents, our sex, the language we were brought up to speak, the culture we were brought up in, the laws of physics. Sartre uses the word 'facticity' to refer to the things that happen to be true of us and that we did not choose. Our facticity is what Sartre is thinking about on page 46 of *E & H* when he refers to our 'limitations'.

One aspect of our facticity, a fact which we can do nothing about, is that we are being-for-itself; we do not have an essence, we are free. This is what Sartre was getting at when he said, 'man is condemned to be free' (*E & H*, p. 34).[49] But it seems a bit odd for Sartre to assert both that:

- We are free.
- We are not free to reject our freedom.

This is sometimes called Sartre's PARADOX OF FREEDOM, because these two assertions seem contradictory, yet Sartre does not want to surrender either one. The paradox and the contradiction disappear once we accept that freedom has limits and that there are plenty of things we cannot choose.

So, in Sartre's view, our facticity does not represent a limitation on our freedom. Rather, our facticity is the framework within which we must express our freedom, through the choices we make in life. Freedom needs facticity, as we cannot act or choose in a vacuum; we need concrete circumstances against which we can act. Freedom occurs in real life between real options which are given to us. So, facticity limits the choices available to us but does not limit freedom. We can illustrate this idea with the analogy of actors on a stage (Figure 5.3).

■ **Figure 5.3**

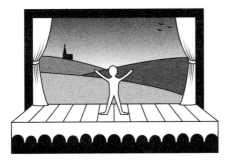

In this analogy the stage furniture and backdrop are controlled by the director. The actors can do nothing about what the scenery is or when it changes; it is their facticity. But, in front of the specific scenery that they have been given as the backdrop to their actions, the actors are free to make whatever choices are available to them. So, in real life, we live in a specific context (physical, social, economic, historical, cultural, biological) which is beyond our control.[50] Our specific context, our facticity, limits the choices that are available to us, but within it we are absolutely free to choose our own attitude to the situation and to make our own decisions.[51] Having a specific context can actually make our actions more meaningful because they gain a direction and a focus.

We might say that our facticity gives us a set of obstacles 障礙物 that limit our freedom. For example, if we are born in a country with a failing economy, we face a difficult life: our financial circumstances are huge obstacles to our projects in life. But it is worth recognising that, for Sartre, in order for us to encounter obstacles in the first place, we must be free. In order to see something as an obstacle, we must first have some project (freely chosen) which it obstructs. For example, the Wright brothers saw our lack of wings as an obstacle to being free to fly, so they invented the aeroplane to overcome that obstacle. Obstacles, things which prevent us from achieving our goals and which are part of our facticity, are not things which get in the way of freedom: we are able see them as obstacles only because we are free in the first place. Our facticity throws our freedom into sharp relief.

experimenting with ideas

Read through the following situations.

a) Given these obstacles, what are all the possible options that someone has?

b) What would your response be to these obstacles?

1 You want to go on holiday with your friends, but you have just lost your job.
2 You have been in a car accident and have lost the use of one of your legs.
3 Your country goes to war and you are conscripted into the army.
4 You have become addicted to painkillers, and can no longer function without them.
5 You are carrying an injured friend through the wilderness to find help, but every step you take hurts you more and more.

There is one other aspect to our lives which we cannot choose, but which gives each of us our individual context: our past. For Sartre, the things we have done in the past are a part of our facticity: we are not free to change them, but they are part of the backdrop against which we act. We may choose to react against our past; we are also free to embrace our past, and to give it value and meaning. But we are not free to go back and to change what we have done. We must accept our past and move on, reinventing ourselves.

This way of describing the human condition has its difficulties.

▶ criticism ◀ On page 48 we saw how even a prisoner locked in chains possesses absolute freedom. Can we ever meaningfully say that such a person is free? Sartre's point is that the prisoner's facticity (which in this case has led to enormous limitations on his physical movement) never actually determines what he says and thinks. But would it not make much more sense to say that the prisoner, in a fundamental way, is not really free at all – never mind what Sartre says about his possessing metaphysical freedom? Is Sartre's metaphysical freedom the kind of freedom we should really be concerned about? There is a danger that other people might shrug their shoulders and say, 'Well, Sartre says that these political prisoners are as free as us, so we don't need to do anything about them.'

Sartre could respond to this criticism by saying that the attitude that we take to our situation is always within our power. So, in the extreme situation of finding ourselves imprisoned, whether we struggle to keep sane or whether we descend into madness is a choice, and an important choice, which we can make. For Sartre, our attitude to life is an important choice, and one which can motivate us to action or lead us to the quietism of despair.

▶ criticism ◀ A second, related, problem is that Sartre does not seem to worry sufficiently about facticity and the very real constraints it imposes on the options that are open to us in our lives. The fact that being a certain sex or class or race (or having no money, or living under an oppressive regime, or being born in a debt-ridden developing country which is forced to grow cash crops and to destroy the land through over-use) limits our possible choices does not trouble Sartre, at least at this stage of his philosophy. But it should trouble us if we wish to evaluate his theory. What is metaphysical freedom worth if someone's possible choices are severely limited by, although allegedly not determined by, their facticity? There is a danger that, if we think only in terms of metaphysical freedom, we may become blasé about the plight of those without social and political freedom.

Evaluation of Sartre's claim that we are free

▶ criticism ◀

Sartre claims that there is nothing common to human beings, no essential human nature which might limit their freedom of choice. We have seen that his argument to this end contrasts the human being with the being of a paper-knife, but we might object that this contrast is misleading. While it is clear that a paper-knife has been produced for a specific purpose, what of other living creatures, such as a dog? Like a human, a dog is not designed to fulfil any specific purpose, and yet it is clear that its behaviour is determined to some degree by its nature. If something is a dog, then it will bark at strangers, chase after sticks and wag its tail. These characteristic behaviours are surely a consequence of the essential nature of dogs. Similarly, people have not been designed for any purpose but are none the less restricted in what they can choose to do by their nature. Human beings are, after all, predictable to some degree, as advertisers and politicians know very well.

▶ criticism ◀

We may well think that Sartre's talk about freedom merely plays with words. In reality, if given the option 'your money or your life' by a robber, our 'freedom' to choose life is not worthy to be called a choice. Sartre, for rhetorical reasons, may be emphasising our fundamental freedom to choose, but the fact remains that we do not always have much of a choice. His position does not really challenge the more normal view that yielding under threat is to be *coerced* rather than to make a truly voluntary action.

Sartre treats human freedom as something absolute and inescapable, but in so doing he divorces the concept from its everyday use and meaning. He leaves no room for the idea that freedom might be a matter of degree which can vary over time, from place to place, and between different individuals.[52] Surely a prisoner confined to a tiny cell has more limited freedom than someone at liberty?

Someone who is addicted to cigarettes seems to have a degree of freedom somewhat less than that of someone who is not. The smoker thinks that they choose to buy each packet and to smoke each cigarette. Yet, in another sense, they are not free because they are physically addicted to nicotine and cannot simply choose to give up. Sartre, for all of his talk of freedom, tried and apparently failed to give up smoking![53]

▶ criticism ◀   An important point, which is not really acknowledged by Sartre, is that factors such as intoxication, fear, illness, emotional insecurity or psychopathology can weaken the control we have over our actions or even remove it altogether. This view of freedom is surely central to our dealings with others and not one to be ignored. In the law, for example, we recognise that the responsibility people have for the choices they make and the actions they perform can be mitigated or limited by circumstances. If someone murders their spouse in a fit of rage, having found them in bed with a lover, we tend to hold them less responsible for their actions than if they had planned the deed with malice aforethought. Why? Because their control over their actions had been diminished and their freedom to choose limited. (No doubt you considered objections to Sartre's account of freedom from this direction when thinking about the scenarios in the activity on page 55.)

▶ criticism ◀   Sartre may also be accused of thinking that the world is composed of white, male, bourgeois Parisians. He does not seem to consider seriously the condition of people for whom social and economic constraints present formidable obstacles, not just in terms of action but also in terms of thinking of themselves as capable of action. In order to be able to act with full freedom, we have to recognise what options are available. This is fine for people brought up and educated in a liberal country where many values are discussed and tolerated. But if we have been brought up to believe that the only real option is to live the life of a dutiful wife, then the possibility of becoming, say, a guerrilla fighter remains closed. These groups may still have choice, according to Sartre's definition, but it is important to recognise that, for them, the range of choices available is significantly restricted.

▶ criticism ◀   We have tried to show that Sartre's conclusion of absolute freedom is based on four key foundations. If these foundations cannot withstand the criticisms of other philosophers, then Sartre's argument will collapse, and with it his justification for saying that we are free. So, a defence must be mounted to show, at the very least, that:
- Nothingness means that we can escape from our past and create our future.
- We do not have any essence or human nature.
- Subjectivity is the most appropriate and robust place to begin philosophy.

How true to the daily experience of our lives is Sartre's view of freedom? Sartre appears to claim that our past choices have no impact on the present options open to us and that in each moment we choose afresh what we are to be. But this does not sit well with the way our lives actually unfold. In theory it may be true that the authors of this book could choose today to devote their energies to becoming astronauts, but that is not experienced as a live option. Their past choices have forged a certain path, which now constrains the future direction that they feel they can take in their careers. So, at a metaphysical level we may well remain free but, as good phenomenologists, we surely ought to recognise that this is not the way in which we experience our lives unfolding.

Sartre's friend and fellow existentialist, Maurice Merleau-Ponty, held a view of freedom which avoided the rather absurd claim that we can choose to radically change the direction of our lives at any time. We can take from Merleau-Ponty at least three points that strengthen the existentialist view of freedom.[54] He argued that:

- A responsible choice is not one that may be overthrown at a whim. If we choose today to train as a geography teacher, that choice will be undermined if we suspect that tomorrow we will give up the teacher training to become a bookmaker at a local dog track.
- Many choices are the first step down a long road. We cannot simply 'choose' to be a teacher or a bookmaker, although we are free to begin an apprenticeship as either. So, our freedom is not powerful enough to turn around our life just like that.
- Sartre confused choice with 'not refusing', and so he was too harsh in his judgement that people were responsible for all aspects of their lives. To choose to be Christian is very different from 'not refusing' Christianity. In the former case, someone has made a considered decision. In the latter case, someone may have been brought up as a Christian, they may not know any different, they may not know that they do not have to be a Christian. To Sartre, Christians are responsible for their Christianity, but to Merleau-Ponty they are not necessarily so. Just because someone is leading a certain kind of life does not mean that they have chosen it, only that they have not rejected it. For Merleau-Ponty, we therefore need to find out more about someone's circumstances before we make a judgement about the aspects of their lives for which they are to be held responsible.

It seems as if Sartre may have overstated his case for absolute freedom because of his historical circumstances. It was essential to his theory of freedom that everyone living through the Second World War had to bear responsibility for what was going on around them. People were free to join the resistance, to become collaborators, to fight or to bury their heads in the sand. In this harsh crucible Sartre forged an unforgiving philosophy of freedom. It was only later that he began to emphasise historical circumstances, as well as freedom of the will, as a factor in individual action.[55]

Key points: Chapter 5

What you need to know about the **metaphysical implications** of the foundations:

1 The four foundations we identified in Chapter 4 have significant consequences for us as human beings.
2 In *B & N*, Sartre's analysis of subjectivity leads him to the conclusion that we are being-for-itself, and as such we have nothingness at the heart of our being. This means that we are able to reject or embrace our past as we wish and to choose our future: in other words, we are absolutely free.
3 In *E & H*, Sartre argues that, because there is no God to have designed humans, we have no essence. Moreover, because there is no God, there are no moral rules or obligations to bind us. This means that we can determine who and what we are: in other words, we are absolutely free.
4 The absolute freedom that Sartre is talking about is not political freedom, but freedom of the will. This means freedom to weigh up possible actions and then to choose one of these possibilities.
5 Sartre believes that many of us do not want this absolute freedom. We do not want to face the responsibility that freedom brings.
6 Absolute freedom does not mean absolute power or omnipotence. Our freedom does have limits, there are things we cannot choose. Sartre refers to these limits as our facticity, and this includes our past, our biology, the laws of nature. Importantly, one of the things we cannot choose is our freedom. It is against this backdrop of our facticity that we are able to act freely.
7 Sartre's account of freedom is very controversial. Most importantly, he does not seem to acknowledge the idea of 'degrees of freedom', for example, between a child and an adult, or between an adult with severe brain damage and an adult with a healthy brain.

6

Emotional implications: Anguish, abandonment and despair

Introduction

Read E & H pages 30–42 and 56

The implications of Sartre's discovery that we are nothingness and have no essence are far-reaching. We have seen what follows metaphysically from this discovery (in terms of what we are really like), namely that we possess absolute free will. We have also begun to sketch people's response to this freedom, often one of fear and denial. But the ramifications of Sartre's theory are even more personal, reaching to our emotions and to our fundamental attitudes to life.

Sartre is amongst the few western philosophers to have given serious philosophical weight to our emotions. One of Sartre's earliest philosophical publications, *Sketch for a Theory of the Emotions* (1939), was an analysis of the phenomenology of human emotions. It was his aim to give a full description of the world as we experience it, and any phenomenological account of the world must include an account of our emotions. It is not surprising, then, that Sartre devotes much of *Existentialism and Humanism* to an analysis of the feelings we have once we realise that we are free. The emotional implications of freedom form the centerpiece of Sartre's lecture and in this chapter and the next we examine our personal response to freedom: the emotions we feel (anguish, abandonment and despair) and the evasive action we take (bad faith). This chapter is divided as follows, each section addressing one of the emotions and a related concept mentioned in Sartre's lecture:

- Anguish and responsibility
- Abandonment and choice
- Despair and quietism
- Key points you need to know about the emotional implications of Sartre's theory.

Anguish and responsibility

What do we mean by anguish? . . . When a man commits himself to anything, fully realising that he is not only choosing what he will be, but is thereby . . . a legislator deciding for the whole of mankind – in such a moment a man cannot escape from the sense of complete and profound responsibility. (E & H, p. 30)

According to Sartre, living with the reality of our absolute freedom is not easy. We do not like to dwell on our freedom, on all of the possible actions we could take, on the sheer enormity of our freedom. We shrink from questions such as 'What am I going to do with my life?', 'What am I going to do today?' or even 'What shall I do now?' because they fill us with fear. But this is not fear of something in the world but fear of something within us, of our freedom and what we might do with it. Existentialists often refer to this fear of freedom as anguish. As Sartre writes, 'fear is fear of beings in the world whereas anguish is anguish before myself' (B & N, p. 29).

Most of the time we avoid dwelling on our anguish by ignoring the fact that we are free. We pretend that we have no real choices: that we must become a lawyer because it is a family tradition; or we must go to school because it's Monday; or we must have breakfast because . . . well, because that is what we do. In other words, we fall into routines and habits in order to avoid facing up to the fact that we are choosing to do all of these things. However, at certain critical times in our lives, we will be confronted once again with the inescapable fact that we are free. At such moments the anguish of freedom reveals itself, as we are brought up sharply against the brutal reality that it is down to us, and only us, to choose what to do next, how to continue with our life.

Sartre extends this anguish to include our fear of responsibility. With freedom comes the realisation that we, and no one else (no God, no nature, no id, no nothing), are actually responsible for our life: for our successes, our failures, our mistakes, our bad decisions, our relationships, even our emotions. But we do not want it, we just cannot handle it, it makes us feel sick, it fills us with angst. So, our anguish arises with our recognition of personal freedom and responsibility.

In *E & H*, Sartre adds yet another dimension to anguish: the anxiety that comes from embracing our responsibility for not only our own actions but also the whole of humanity's. This may seem extreme, and if it were true it would certainly deepen our anxiety about freedom. In Chapter 8 we shall look at exactly how Sartre draws this conclusion. For now, let us just dwell on this aspect of anguish: whatever we choose to do, we must take responsibility for everyone who decides to do the same thing. It is as if we were a celebrity and everything we did were reported in the tabloid press and imitated by hordes of fans. So, if we lie, we must take responsibility when other people lie; if we have an affair with someone who is married, we must take responsibility for the infidelities of others. In the next chapter we shall see how most of us avoid anguish, by pretending that we are not free and are not responsible.

One problem thrown up by Sartre's concept of anguish is this: if we are free and responsible all the time, why do we not feel anguish all the time?[56] Sartre's answer is that we disguise or bury the anguish by pretending to ourselves that we are not free. Think of a man who has just heard of the death of his mother. Instead of grieving and letting out his pain, he carries on as if nothing has happened, as if he feels nothing. This is our response to anguish: we pretend that freedom is not a part of our lives when in fact it is unavoidable. We shall look at this self-denial or deception in Chapter 7.

ACTIVITY Read pages 31–2 of *E & H* and explain in what way each of the following people might be in anguish:

1 Abraham, who was commanded by an angel to kill his son Isaac on a mountaintop as a sacrifice to God.
2 A mad woman who is given orders by telephone by someone claiming to be God.
3 An officer who sends his men to their death in battle, following a command from higher up.

Abandonment and choice

When we speak of 'abandonment' . . . we only mean to say that God does not exist, and that it is necessary to draw the consequences of his absence right to the end.
(E & H, *pp. 32–3)*

There is another kind of terrible emotion that we must face on our journey to freedom. It arises from the realisation that there is no God, no purpose, nothing which can support us in this cruel world.

When we are growing up we often believe, or are told, that there is a purpose to life or some kind of meaning to existence. It is very comforting to believe that an external authority exists, someone who is there to look after us, to support us, to give purpose to our lives and to dish out justice when we die. We also start to believe that we have an essence, either one that all humans share – human nature – or one peculiar to ourselves – a personality or set of character traits.

Then something happens; it could be something traumatic, such as losing a loved one or being made redundant, or else attending a philosophy class or reading one of Sartre's stories. Gradually we start to look at the world differently. We may see it as meaningless, no longer finding any point or purpose to it. For Sartre, this occurs because we have made an existential realisation: we have recognised that we have no essence, that there is no God, and that there is no divine plan conferring meaning on the world or offering guidance on how we should live.[57]

What implications does this atheism have for our understanding and experience of the world? In the passage from *Nausea* on pages 23–4, Roquentin began to see material objects, specifically the roots of a tree, in a new way. Suddenly he was struck by the brute fact of their existence. Here were objects which just exist. But why? What is the meaning of their existing? Roquentin could fathom no purpose or meaning in such existence and was deeply disturbed by a recognition of the fundamental absurdity and pointlessness of the things in the world. He saw them as superfluous. When we think about the enormity of the world, and how it is a result of some mindless accident, does it not also strike us as *absurd*? What is the point of it all? It might just as well have been the case that the Earth remained a primal soup with no living being of any kind. In *B & N*, Sartre looks at how our first reaction to the world, as we start to recognise the pointlessness of existence for the first time, is one of disgust at its meaninglessness. But this disgust is quickly replaced by a more profound emotion: the feeling of *abandonment* that overwhelms us when we realise that there is no God, that the world is meaningless, and that we can choose to do anything.

Why does Sartre use such an emotive and strong term as 'abandonment'? Abandonment is really a metaphor, since, to an atheist such as Sartre, there never was a God to have abandoned us. Rather, it is as if we have had a revelation and seen that our belief in God (or any sort of external purpose) was wrong and must be given up.[58] So, although God has never existed, we still feel deeply the loss of the security brought by the idea of God. A rather weak analogy is that of a child who realises on Christmas Eve that Santa Claus does not exist. However, existential abandonment is much worse: the foundation for life's meaning and morality, in which we once had faith and trust, has now disappeared. That makes us feel alone, abandoned. We are abandoned in so many ways if there is no God. As well as having no essence or purpose, we no longer have moral commandments to guide us through our lives. We are left only with our own choices with which to shape our lives.

Sartre believes that ultimately it falls to us individually to overcome our feelings of abandonment, absurdity, and disgust. In *Nausea*, Roquentin's feelings of disgust at the absurdity and meaninglessness of the universe are only a step on the way to a recognition that if there is to be meaning and purpose in life it is we who must create them. Just because there is no God telling us how to live does not mean that there is no point in living. Rather, it means that we have to face up to the task of constructing purpose and values for ourselves. For example, if we go to the park to play football, but discover that there are no goalposts in position, we could spend ages looking for them without success and then leave the park feeling cheated and abandoned. Alternatively, we could make our own goalposts (with jumpers, say) and get on with the game.

ACTIVITY   Read pages 35–8 of *E & H*. Here Sartre gives the famous example of a pupil of his who comes to him for advice: should he stay at home to look after his mother, or should he join the French resistance to avenge his brother's death? Sartre cannot help him.

a) What do you think of Sartre's reaction to the pupil? Would you have reacted differently if the pupil had come to you for advice?
b) Which course of action would you take if you were Sartre's pupil? Why?

Abandonment is the position in which Sartre's pupil finds himself when faced with this awful dilemma. There is nothing and no one to help him to make this difficult moral decision. It is up to the pupil to determine for himself, independently of any advice or support, what his purpose in life is. It is also up to the pupil to make his own moral choices, as he cannot draw on any objective morality for guidance. Even if he were lucky enough to be a student of moral philosophy and so armed with Christian, Kantian or utilitarian ethical theories, these would still be of no help in a concrete situation. This goes for all of us. Ultimately we have to interpret the theory and decide in what way it applies here, for us: and this is a choice. For Sartre, all of our moral values are invented in the choices and actions we take. So, if the pupil decides to stay with his mother, then, by making that choice, he values his mother above his country. If he decides to join the Free

French resistance abroad, then that choice means that he values his country above his mother. The pupil must make his choice alone; as Sartre said to him: 'You are free, therefore choose – that is to say, invent' (*E & H*, p. 38).

▶ criticism ◀ What is involved in a freely chosen act? Sartre often talks about people (or being-for-itself) as inventing and making themselves through their actions. This is because we are not determined by our past, our nature or our personality; we are free. The pupil is a vivid example of someone in the process of inventing themselves through their freely chosen action. Is the pupil to be someone who puts his family first, or someone who puts his country or humanity first? Sartre makes it clear that there is nothing that can help the pupil to decide what sort of person he should be or what course of action he should take. There are no advisors he can rely on, no signs he can look for, no moral codes to guide him. Sartre even says that the pupil's feelings are of no help, because how do we measure the strength of one feeling against another? The problem is, if nothing is to act as a motivator for the pupil's action, where does the act come from? If it cannot be based on internal reasons, or on emotions, or on external factors, then what is the decision based on? Is the pupil's act simply arbitrary? Sartre again says no, as he rejects the idea (put forward by Gide) that genuine choice is based on a whim.[59] It seems, then, as if Sartre cannot say what a freely chosen action is. Sartre's pupil seems to be abandoned not just by God but also by philosophy![60]

The problem arises because Sartre refuses to analyse just what freedom is, or where it comes from. Other philosophers across the ages, such as Aristotle and Hume, have been willing to offer theories of the mind which account for decision making and even try to explain what a freely chosen act is. Of course Sartre, because he takes a phenomenological approach, can only grapple with freedom 'from the inside', in other words, from our experience of free choice. Sartre can therefore tell us what is *not* a free action (one where we let ourselves be influenced by advisors, signs, values, feelings), but he cannot say what *is* a free action.[61] However, Sartre's position is more complicated than this. He thinks that there is no such thing as an 'unfree action'. Since freedom is unavoidable for humans, Sartre would say that even if we let our actions be guided by advice, signs or moral rules, we are still freely choosing to follow such guidance. We cannot escape our free choice, and any attempt we make to escape freedom is an act of self-deception (as we shall see in the next chapter).

Anguish and abandonment are not the only emotions that we face when we first encounter freedom on our journey of existential enlightenment. The next emotion that Sartre addresses in *E & H* is despair. Like anguish and abandonment, despair is an emotion with which we have to deal as long as we are alive. With courage, we can live with all of these negative emotions and still embrace our freedom.

Despair and quietism

As for 'despair', the meaning of this expression is extremely simple. It merely means that we limit ourselves to a reliance upon that which is within our wills. (E & H, p. 39)

When we were younger, we were constantly frustrated by the way in which the world refused to bend itself to our will. People, and things, just did not do what we wanted them to do: pigeons we tried to play with would fly away; the hateful green chewy stuff would keep appearing on our dinner plate; distant objects would not magically fall into our grasp simply because we reached out for them and wailed. As we grew up, we learned to manage our frustration, to realise that not everything is within our power, and to understand that sometimes we have to sit back and see the world as beyond our control. Sartre calls this feeling of impotence and helplessness 'despair'. It can have either a positive or a negative effect on our lives. The positive side is that we can learn to focus our efforts on what is within our power. The negative side is that we may come to think that most things in the world are beyond our control, giving rise to a new and crippling attitude: quietism. For Sartre, we must live in despair whilst avoiding quietism. Let us look at both despair and quietism in more detail.

Despair is the emotion we feel when we recognise that aspects of the world are beyond us – that there is nothing we can do about them. Perhaps we are fuming because we are stuck on a train, or because someone is late or because a sudden downpour has just drenched us. Our projects are constantly being frustrated, but we must just deal with this. Crucial to the existentialist attitude of despair is that we must realise not only that much of the world is out of our control but also, more importantly, that there is no God who is going to step in and assist us. For many people this brings real despair. Whether we are faced with trivial matters, perhaps standing in a slow-moving queue, or with hugely significant ones, perhaps a loved one dying of an incurable disease, we must live in despair. In other words, we must live in the knowledge that, with some things, there is nothing we can do, and there is no God who will help us in answer to our prayers. However, for Sartre, despair gives us a new attitude to life. It reveals to us that we should be committed to do what we can do and should not worry about what we cannot. So, if our train is late, instead of swearing, we should go and find out what has happened to it and when it is due. Once we have done all that we are able to do, and there is nothing more we can do, we should stop fretting about the train.

In the final few words of the lecture, Sartre revisits the despair of existentialism and he subtly refines his position. (It is worth noting Sartre's play on words – *deséspoir*: despair; *désespérés*: desperate – to produce a neat final flourish to his lecture.)

And if by despair one means – as the Christians do – any attitude of unbelief, the despair of the existentialists is something different . . . [Existentialism] is a doctrine of action, and it is only by self-deception, by confounding their own despair [deséspoir] with ours that Christians can describe us as without hope [désespérés]. (E & H, *p.* 56)

Sartre says that his intention is not to plunge people into despair; existentialist despair does not mean giving up on life, as Christians imply it does. Instead, it means getting on with our life's projects without worrying about the things that we cannot change. Although existentialist despair is atheistic (because there is no God to answer our prayers), for Sartre this does not mean that existentialists are obsessed with proving that God does not exist. Nor does it mean that they are 'desperate' as the Christians say, namely, searching for a God or a meaning that their lives lack. For the existentialists, whether or not there is a God, we must still decide for ourselves what to do with our lives, and we must still deal with our freedom alone. Despair is part and parcel of our freedom. However, despair has a dangerous side for Sartre. Sometimes it seems that so much of the world is beyond our control that there is nothing we can do. When too much of the world seems out of reach, when our despair becomes unbearable, then we may sink into inaction and apathy. This is a state Sartre calls 'quietism'.

One route from despair to quietism springs from our attitude to death: if, after we die, it is possible that everything we have done will be undone, then what is the point? This is particularly true for people who want to change the world in order to improve it. What can one individual do about poverty and starvation in developing countries? Or about the possible revival of fascism in the future? Why do anything if all our efforts eventually come to nothing after we are dead?

So, if we cannot control the world, then we may sit back and do nothing, and instead be happy thinking that others are struggling to change the world, to create great art, to live the best possible life. But from Sartre's existentialist position, this is a very dangerous attitude, because we are the sum of our actions, and nothing more. There are no 'secret talents' hidden inside us: if we have achieved nothing, then that is all that we are: someone who has achieved nothing. Sartre gives the example of someone who is full of excuses about why they have not achieved what they could have achieved (*E & H*, p. 41). The excuses are never about them, but always about the world. We all know someone who says, 'I could have been a great writer/footballer/A level student/politician but I never had a lucky break,' when the real reason for their failure is that they could not get their act together. Such people hope for their situation to change without having to do anything about it themselves (such as actually writing a book). This kind of hope also involves a denial of one's freedom: a self-deceiving desire to be subject to forces beyond one's control. It is an unnecessary luxury indulged in by those who cannot face up to the harsh realities of the human condition; by those who would rather sit around dreaming of the fine things they could do, rather than actually doing them.

So, quietism springs from despair, as the world seems out of our reach. But quietism provides us with no comfort, and its temptations lead to a pathetic and unfulfilling life.

It is easy to see why Sartre is criticised for being depressing and for encouraging a pessimistic 'why bother?' attitude to the world (*E & H*, p. 23); after all, he has painted rather a despondent picture of the world so far, full of anguish, abandonment and despair. But Sartre attacks quietism as it goes against his fundamental claim that, because we are free, 'Man is nothing else . . . but the sum of his actions' (*E & H*, p. 41).

We must learn to recognise the limits of our will, learn to identify those features of the world that we can do something about and those that we cannot. We must not get frustrated about what is beyond us, however, or cease to care about what is within our power. What we can do something about we must do something about, what we cannot do something about we must leave. This is not a doctrine of quietism, or an excuse to see the world as beyond us. We must act, and if we cannot act in one way we should not despair since there are plenty of other ways in which we can act.

 *experimenting with ideas*

Read through the following situations and for each of them identify whether the person is feeling anguish, abandonment or despair (or quietism).

1 Zac has just left college, having passed her City and Guilds in plumbing, the last time she will ever sit an exam. The world is her oyster, but she needs to chill out for a bit. She spends the summer in a daze of late-night partying, clubbing and hedonism. She even recreates a small corner of Ibiza in her back garden with some builders' sand and some carefully placed bottles. She had planned to go travelling round the world as a plumber, footloose and fancy free, but does not manage to get it together to find a job. Come September, she is back in college, seeking to study for any advanced diploma. (*What feeling causes Zac to go back to college?*)

2 Nadine has become obsessed with sport. She watches it on TV every day as soon as she gets up and as soon as she returns home from work. Golf, wrestling, Australian rules football; no matter the sport, she watches it all. One day, she has settled down for a twelve-hour session. Ten minutes into the opening ceremony, the TV packs in. After punching the wall a few times, Nadine falls back on to the sofa. She remains there for the rest of the day, staring at the blank screen, unable to move. (*What state is Nadine in after the TV breaks?*)

3 Soraya works at an exclusive fashion house, called *La femme*, designing handmade clothes. Her range of clothing shapes the world of fashion, everyone loves her work and everyone imitates it. One day her muse, an impossibly tall and thin model, is killed in a freak accident. Soraya breaks down in tears as she realises that, with her muse gone, her work is now pointless – the clothes she makes fit only this tall, thin model. 'We're all going to die!' she bawls, to anyone who will listen, and she locks herself into her panic room. (*What does Soraya feel when her model dies?*)

4 Krikor is having an argument with his dad. 'It's nothing to do with me. I wasn't even there. I was asleep.' Earlier in the week he had been dropping water bombs from the top balcony of their block of flats – a bit of harmless fun. His little sister, Sabrina, had seen him do this from her bedroom and had told on him. Today Krikor's parents were walking home from their early morning swim when a hamster whistled past their ears and hit the ground. They looked up and saw Sabrina on the top balcony. (*What is Krikor feeling when he argues with his dad?*)

5 Pierre faces a terrible dilemma. Both options available to him will bring him and his family grief and hardship, but he has to choose one of them. He thinks long and hard about what to do, weighing up the pros and cons of each choice, but he cannot decide. He would like to do both, but he is scared of doing either. He decides to ask the one person who could be of genuine help to him, his philosophy professor, whom he both admires and respects. After ten minutes of waffling, the professor stops and waves Pierre goodbye. Apparently the professor has friends and a black coffee waiting for him at Les Deux Magots, the local café. Pierre sits on the steps of the university in amazement – he has never heard his professor be so fatuous, so pretentious and so vague. The meeting has been a complete waste of time, he might as well have gone to see his local doctor, Monsieur Petiot, who has always seemed more helpful. (*What state does Pierre realise he is in after visiting the professor?*)

What you need to know about the **emotional implications** of Sartre's theory:

1 In all of his works Sartre places high value on our emotional experience of the world. In *E & H*, Sartre identifies three emotions at the heart of his existentialist account of human experience: anguish, abandonment and despair. These are the emotions with which, because we are free beings, we must live until we die.

2 Anguish is a state in which all humans live, whether we are aware of it or not. It is the nauseating fear that we have when we realise that we are not only free but also responsible for all of our actions. In *E & H*, Sartre adds a further reason for our anguish: our responsibility for the whole of humanity when we commit ourselves to action. It is as if, whenever we act, the eyes of the world are upon us.

3 Abandonment arises when we recognise that there is no God. The lack of any external authority who can look after us and give our lives purpose is extremely shocking. We feel alone. But it is in that state of loneliness that we must make decisions about how to act. There is no one to help or guide us, and so we must invent our values for ourselves.

4 Sartre's pupil was abandoned. No one could help him to make his decision. There were no advisors to whom he could turn, no moral theory to guide him, no signs that would show him the way. Even his own feelings could not tell him for certain which decision he should make. The problem is that Sartre cannot clearly explain on what his (or our) free choices should be based.

5 The final emotion we must live with is despair. This is the feeling of frustration and impotence we have when things are beyond our control. It would be great if there were a God to whom we could pray and who would change the world to suit us. But there is no God and so we just have to deal with the fact that certain things are beyond us. This is despair.

6 Despair can lead us to focus on what is within our power: we direct our attention on the things we can do, and ignore what we cannot. However, despair can also lead to quietism, which is the attitude of surrender to life. Quietism means giving up on action because everything seems pointless, or unavoidable or out of our control. It is important to Sartre that we reject quietism because we are nothing but the sum of our actions.

7
Ethical implications: Bad faith, authenticity and other people

Introduction

Read *E & H* pages 30–1, 44–5, 50–1

Sartre never produced a fully-fledged moral theory. It may seem odd even to expect him to have written one. After all, here was a man who condemned people who believed in objective moral values, calling such a belief the 'SPIRIT OF SERIOUSNESS'.[62] Moreover, here was a man who espoused the view that, if there is no God, then we can do whatever we like. This is hardly the talk of a moral philosopher, and sounds very close to NIHILISM: the rejection of all values.

But Sartre did have values and he acted on them – he fought for his fellow countrymen; he condemned the actions of the Nazis and the French collaborators; he campaigned against French war crimes in Algeria and American war crimes in Vietnam. These are not the actions of someone who rejects all moral values. In fact, one of the struggles Sartre faced throughout his intellectual life was reconciling two deeply held, and apparently incompatible, values, whilst avoiding the 'spirit of seriousness'. On the one hand, Sartre placed value on the authentic, free choices that individuals make for themselves; on the other, he believed that we should value the freedom not just of ourselves but also of all other individuals. The second of these values is particularly troubling for an existentialist. After all, if we are free, and if there is no God to lay down the moral law, then why should we value anything that does not benefit ourselves? Sartre's search for reconciliation of these two values eventually led him away from existentialism and towards Marxism.

We are concerned here with morality as it relates to Sartre's existentialism. He never actually wrote and published a work specifically on moral philosophy. However, we can find glimpses of his moral thinking in his work: he did talk about writing an existentialist moral theory in *Being and Nothingness*; he sketched a moral theory in *Existentialism and Humanism*; he even wrote extensive notes on such a theory for years after the lecture. Chapters 7 and 8 examine the relationship between ethics and existentialism. In Chapter 7 we look at the implications for morality as they can be found in *B & N*; in Chapter 8 we look at the moral theory put forward by Sartre in *E & H*.

Sartre does not explicitly mention ethics in *B & N*, except in the infamous and much discussed footnote that occurs at the end of a depressing chapter on our relationships with other people:

These considerations do not exclude the possibility of an ethics of deliverance and salvation. But this can be achieved only after a radical conversion which we cannot discuss here. (B & N, *p. 412*)

At the end of *B & N*, Sartre promised a future work on ethics, one which might have dealt with this 'radical conversion'. Unfortunately he did not keep this promise, and the radical conversion he himself underwent was towards Marxism. We are left to work out for ourselves what Sartre's purely existential ethics might have been. We are helped in this by three things:

- *B & N* itself can be seen as offering a kind of existential morality.
- We find clues throughout *E & H* to the direction Sartre might have taken to construct an existentialist ethics.
- Although Sartre (unlike Simone de Beauvoir)[63] never actually published a work on existential ethics, he did write his thoughts in a series of notebooks, two of which have now been published as *Notebooks for an Ethics*.

We have just said that Sartre does not explicitly propose an existentialist ethics in *B & N*, but is it implicit in this work? In its widest sense ethics is concerned with how we should live our lives, and in particular how we should treat others. If a theory is ethical when it addresses both of these issues, then it may be possible to conclude that Sartre's existentialism, even prior to *E & H*, is an ethical theory. We can say this for three reasons.

- Sometimes, in spite of himself, Sartre does tell us how we should live our lives; we shall look at this in the sections below on bad faith (page 74) and authenticity (page 83).
- Although Sartre does not tell us how we *should* treat other people, he certainly goes into a lot of detail about how we inevitably *do* treat other people; this is dealt with in the section below on other people (page 85).
- Mary Warnock has argued[64] that every form of existentialism can be seen as a moral theory, even when there is no mention of ethics. This is because existentialism demands that we take a certain attitude to the world. It is

not concerned with an analysis of the world as it really is, or with finding objective knowledge, or with giving us better conceptual understanding. Sartre does engage in conceptual analysis, but this is just to lay the groundwork for a more important project. A philosophy based on subjectivity is a philosophy that tells us to search for meaning for ourselves. Sartre's theory makes demands on us to transform our lives, our behaviour and our actions. It asks us to think about how we live, and to change. And so it is possible, despite Sartre's vagueness about an existential moral theory, to see the whole of Sartre's existentialism as a moral project.

The rest of this chapter is divided as follows:

- Bad faith ⎱ How we should live our lives
- Authenticity ⎰
- Other people ⎱ How we should treat others
- Intersubjectivity ⎰
- Key points you need to know about the ethical implications of Sartre's theory.

Bad faith

One of the most compelling aspects of Sartre's existentialism is his account of bad faith or SELF-DECEPTION. It is described in great detail in *B & N* and he touches on it throughout *E & H*. There are strong connections between bad faith and ethics, even though these connections are not explicitly drawn out by Sartre. For Sartre, bad faith represents our failure to live our lives in the right kind of way. Those of us in bad faith have taken the wrong attitude to our freedom and Sartre is quick to condemn such people in a manner which smacks of moralising. Even though Sartre does not tell us what we should do with our lives, he does tell us what attitude we should take to our lives. In this sense, then, bad faith is part of Sartre's moral project.

What is bad faith?

We have seen that, as self-conscious beings, we have absolute freedom. Sartre claims that we are actually aware of this freedom all the time because we are always subject to a kind of anguish – the minor kind that we have when we realise that we are free to do anything, but must take responsibility. However, it is only in certain circumstances (losing a job, bereavement, an accident – something that makes us examine our life) that we feel anguish. How can it be the case that we are always in anguish, yet feel it only sometimes?

The answer is, of course, that we pretend not to notice our anguish. We do all that we can to avoid the knowledge, which we certainly possess, that we are absolutely free and responsible. In other words, we deliberately deceive ourselves about the extent of our freedom. This deception means that, whilst we know 'deep down' that we are free, we manage to pretend that we do not have any choice in much of our lives. Sartre calls this pretence MAUVAISE FOI, literally meaning 'bad faith' but commonly translated as 'self-deception'.

By living in bad faith we do, of course, evade the terrible responsibility of having to make decisions about our lives; we simply follow the rules. If we so choose, we could wake up tomorrow and behave differently, start using different words, dress differently, get a different job, leave the town we live in. If we are free, there is nothing to prevent us from reinventing ourselves tomorrow, and the next day, and the next day, and the next. But it is much simpler to pretend that we have an essence, to say, 'I'm the sort of person who doesn't do this or that' or 'I'm always on time for work' or 'I have a mortgage, I can't just change my life.' Our lives are easier when we pretend that we have no choice, that we are determined by an 'essence'. But Sartre thinks that he has shown that we are free, that we have no essence and that we are deluding ourselves by pretending to have one.

Pick a friend you know really well and imagine them in the following situation.

Your friend is walking home alone late one summer's evening after a delightful barbecue with friends in the suburbs. The sun is setting, the streets are quiet, a pleasant breeze is blowing. Turning a corner, your friend sees a person lying face down on the pavement.

1 What do you think your friend would do in this situation? Why?
2 Now go and ask what your friend would actually do.
3 Were you correct in your prediction?
4 Could your friend have behaved differently? How difficult would this have been for your friend?

Examples of bad faith in *E & H*

In the English version of the lecture, bad faith is translated throughout as 'self-deception'. Sartre discusses it specifically in places, and hints at it in other parts of his lecture. Below are eight ways, drawn mostly from *E & H*, in which Sartre thinks that we can fall into bad faith.

◼ 1 Anguish leads to bad faith

According to Sartre, we feel anguish when we realise the full extent of our responsibility, not just for us but for the whole of humanity. This is a pretty frightening thought, and most of us would gladly pretend that it were not true (if it is indeed true). However, if it is true, then 'one [cannot] escape from that disturbing thought except by a kind of self-deception' (*E & H*, p. 31).

We can avoid anguish by pretending that we are not responsible for our actions, by finding excuses, by blaming others.

◼ 2 Cowards and scum are in bad faith

Sartre mentions two common types of people who deliberately live in denial of their freedom: the cowards and the scum.

I can form judgements upon those who seek to hide from themselves the wholly voluntary nature of their existence and its complete freedom. Those who hide from this total freedom, in a guise of solemnity or with deterministic excuses, I shall call cowards. Others, who try to show that their existence is necessary, when it is merely an accident of the appearance of the human race on earth, – I shall call scum. (E & H, p. 52)

Cowards flee from freedom; they hide in the pretence that they have an essence, that they are being-in-itself. In *B & N*, Sartre devotes twenty pages to a discussion and illustration of this kind of bad faith.[65] He also seems to imply in *B & N* that deep down all of us are in bad faith, because all of us wish to believe that we have some kind of essence.[66]

There are four types of coward:

- Some people choose to live according to the past, identifying themselves with what they used to be, and refusing to move beyond this. They see themselves as having a fixed personality, an unchanging character, which limits their options.
- Some people refuse to step outside of the roles that others have cast for them. These people take on and play their roles as if they had no other choice – the student, the thief, the angry young man, the little sister, the feminist, the waiter, the parent. We all play roles, trying to satisfy others when we should be thinking about what we can freely do.

- Some people absorb themselves, like human robots, in the tiny details of life – their actions are mere superficial gestures, they are not engaged or involved in them. These people attach importance to the banality of everyday life, and they reduce their lives to mechanically acting out their roles.[67]
- Other people exhibit the most extreme version of cowardice, pretending that they are just an object, a being-in-itself, and that they are no more than the flesh and bones of their body. In *B & N*, Sartre gives a persuasive illustration of someone who denies their freedom in this way. In this example a woman on a date is being propositioned by a man, and she is pretending not to notice. Then he takes her hand in his, and she has to make a decision: to leave it there, and thus give tacit consent to his proposal, or to withdraw, and so give him the brush-off. In an act of supreme bad faith she disengages herself from her hand, treating it as if it were not hers, refusing to use it to make a decision.[68] But, of course, we cannot pretend that our bodies are 'things', or that we are objects. For Sartre, even a refusal to act or to choose is a choice; and so the woman, by leaving her hand where it is, is making a choice. We cannot ignore the responsibility we have for the actions of our bodies: they are our actions. To pretend otherwise is bad faith.

experimenting with ideas

1 Write down some examples of people you know who are cowards in Sartre's sense of the word.

2 What roles do you think you play (at home, at college, at work)? Could you change your behaviour patterns in these situations if you wanted to?

We can understand Sartre's use of 'coward' to describe people who run in fear from their freedom. But Sartre defines as 'scum' those people who think of their existence as necessary, as opposed to being accidental (*E & H*, p. 52), and who therefore think that their lives possess an inherent value. Such a belief is certainly bad faith, as we are all without an essence or design or purpose: our existence is pure accident. But to say that people who believe in this are 'scum' is very harsh language for an offence that seems quite minor. It could be that Sartre was thinking of the Nazis when he used the word 'scum': part of the Nazi ideology was their belief that they were part of an Aryan 'master race', who were destined to rule the world.[69] So it is possible that Sartre's mention of cowards and scum as examples of bad faith was influenced by the post-war context of the lecture. Sartre may have wished to point a finger at the Nazis and their collaborators and say:

'You claimed that you were superior to others, and you slavishly followed the myth that you had invented. But you all refused to recognise what you knew to be true – that you were free and could have acted differently.'

ACTIVITY Read page 34 of *E & H* (from 'man is condemned to be free') and answer the following questions.

1 What are two excuses that we use to avoid responsibility?
2 What does the authentic existentialist believe about these excuses?

■ 3 Blaming our actions on our emotions is bad faith

On page 34 of *E & H*, Sartre rejects the view that we can blame our actions on our emotions or 'passions'. If this is true, then it can never be possible for our emotional state to directly cause our physical actions. This is very controversial, as we hold in law that emotions can count for mitigating circumstances. For example, feelings of grief or abuse may lead to an extreme action for which we are not later held fully responsible. Yet Sartre believes that we are responsible for our emotions (or passions), and to say otherwise is bad faith.

 experimenting with ideas

Are people responsible for actions they perform if they are sad? What if they are clinically depressed? What if they have just witnessed their families being murdered?

■ 4 Believing that our life or actions are determined is bad faith

Since we have defined the situation of man as one of free choice . . . any man who takes refuge behind the excuse of his passions, or by inventing some deterministic doctrine, is a self-deceiver. (E & H, pp. 50–1)

Determinism is the view that every event and every action is caused by some prior event; in other words, that nothing could be different from how it actually is, and that our actions are simply the result of some preceding set of circumstances. Determinism can be found in many forms (see, for example, the activity on page 52) and Sartre is an enemy of all of them. We might argue that our actions are determined by our biology; by the physical laws of the universe; by some spiritual fate or karma; by our upbringing or socio-economic class; or by the character and personality with which we were born. Once again, Sartre would say that we believe these things in order to avoid the anguish of choice and responsibility.

How does Sartre explain why some people are, for example, cowards whilst others are courageous? If our characters are not determined by our past, then how are they formed? On page 43 of *E & H*, Sartre explains that a person is not born a coward, and is not a coward because of a cowardly heart or lungs. Cowardice is not a 'given', something inevitable or determined by an essential part of the person. To say that would be to deny their freedom and to pretend that they had an essence, which is bad faith. Sartre argues that the reason why someone is called a coward is because of the cowardly things they have done. They are the sum of their actions, and at the moment their actions add up to cowardliness, but they are free to reinvent themselves as heroic in the future by choosing courageous actions.

5 Blaming our circumstances is bad faith

A good excuse for why we have failed to do something is to blame our situation. On page 41 of *E & H*, Sartre describes someone like Marlon Brando's failed boxer in the film *On the Waterfront*, who says that he 'could have been a contender'.[70] Sartre's character says that 'Circumstances have been against me, I was worthy to be something much better than I have been . . . if I have not written any very good books, it is because I had not the leisure to do so.'

For Sartre, circumstances are no excuse; the reason why this person is not a writer is not because they have been busy, but because they have not chosen to write anything. They could have given up their job, bought some paper and a pen, and spent twelve hours a day writing. But they have not done this, and instead blame their situation.[71] For Sartre, we must accept full responsibility for all of our previous decisions which have led to our present situation.

6 Using 'signs' as an excuse is bad faith

People sometimes feel that there are signs in the world which tell them what to do and guide them through their lives. For example, the Scottish nobleman Robert the Bruce had failed on three occasions in his rebellion against the English. It is said that he was hiding in a cave, about to give up, when he saw a spider trying to make a web; it too failed three times but was successful on the fourth. Robert the Bruce took this as a sign to continue with his struggle to overthrow English rule. Sartre says that we choose to interpret things in the world as signs, and we choose to follow them. We can follow signs in good faith so long as we acknowledge our choice to follow them. Both Abraham and the mad woman (on page 31 of *E & H*) chose to interpret the voices they heard as coming from God and so must accept responsibility for their choice.

On page 38 of *E & H*, Sartre tells us of a man who was a failure in everything he did. One day it occurred to him that his failure was a sign that he was not meant for worldly success, and so he became a priest. For Sartre, the man chose to interpret his failure in this way, and so he really chose to become a priest.

■ 7 Following other people's advice can lead to bad faith

Like Sartre's pupil (on page 35 of *E & H*), we can ask others for advice. But we often turn to others when we cannot make a choice for ourselves, and if we blame them for giving us the wrong advice then we are in bad faith. After all, we have a number of people to whom we can turn for advice – but we choose whom we actually ask. We also have the choice to take their advice. On page 37 of *E & H*, Sartre says that his pupil could have chosen a priest to ask for advice, but instead he chose his philosophy teacher – so he had already selected the range of advice to which he was prepared to listen. Had he chosen a priest, he could have gone to one who was a collaborator with the Germans, or to one who had sympathies with the resistance. Again, his choice of advisor would have revealed the kind of advice that he wanted. So, we choose our advisors and must take full responsibility for following their advice.

■ 8 Belief in objective morality is bad faith

Believing in objective moral values is another form of bad faith. We are completely free – there is no God – and so to pretend that we are bound by a moral 'law' is to deceive ourselves. We shall look at this in more detail in Chapter 8.

Problems with Sartre's concept of bad faith

experimenting with ideas

Mary Warnock suggests that bad faith is sometimes good.[72]
    Can you think of any situations in which it is positively beneficial for people to act in bad faith?

Sartre, in *E & H* and even more so in *B & N*, is adamant in his condemnation of those who act in bad faith. But there are two interrelated problems with his attack on bad faith:

■ What's wrong with someone consciously choosing to act in bad faith, choosing to be a coward or scum?
■ From what moral high ground can Sartre condemn those in bad faith?

▶ criticism ◀ If Sartre is right in asserting that there are no objective moral values, then surely he cannot make any sort of moral judgement, such as 'it is wrong to act in bad faith'? Even calling people who are in bad faith 'cowards' or 'scum' is a value judgement.[73] Moreover, Sartre does not appear to be saying 'oh, and that's only my opinion'. In other words, he is not claiming that his views are subjective. Instead, his attacks seem to come from a moral high ground which, by his own admittance, does not exist.[74] So, can Sartre really tell us why we should not be spineless cowards who refuse to acknowledge our freedom? For Sartre's answer to this question, read pages 50–1 of *E & H*.

One may object: 'But why should he not choose to deceive himself?' I reply that it is not for me to judge him morally, but I define his self-deception as an error. (E & H, p. 51)

Here Sartre reveals that he is not making a moral judgement by condemning people in bad faith, but is making what he calls a 'logical judgement'. In other words, he is attacking them for basing their actions on an error. Their error is pretending that they are not free. So, Sartre's criticism is like the one we would make of people who said they believed that the Earth was round, but who refused to board a ship because they were scared they would fall off the edge of the Earth. The mistake is to base our belief on something we know to be false. So, Sartre avoids contradicting himself by asserting that *mauvaise foi* does not mean morally bad faith, but mistaken faith. Are you convinced? If you are, then how can you explain Sartre's statement, in the middle of page 51 of *E & H*, that 'Furthermore, I can pronounce a moral judgement'? We shall come back to this in Chapter 8 when we look in more detail at his moral theory.

▶ criticism ◀ Sartre's idea of bad faith is usually translated as 'self-deception'. But is the concept of self-deception a coherent one? In order to deceive someone, we must persuade that person to believe something that we think is not true. But what has to happen in order to deceive ourselves? For self-deception to work, we must persuade ourselves to believe something that we think is not true! A simple example of self-deception might involve putting a coin in our right hand, then closing our eyes and trying to believe that the coin is in our left hand. It just does not seem possible. If bad faith is a type of self-deception, then we have to pretend that we are not free when we know that in fact we are.[75]

We have seen one possible solution on page 51 of *E & H*. Here Sartre explains that our self-deception is an error and this may explain why he uses the term 'bad' faith. So, another way of thinking about the phrase is as 'mistaken faith'. In other words, we are putting our faith in a belief which deep down we know is wrong: the belief that we are not free.

This solution implies that self-deception works on an unconscious level. Subconsciously we know that we are free, but at the same time we are not consciously aware of this. George Orwell, in his novel *1984*, invents the similar phenomenon of 'doublethink': 'Doublethink means the power of holding two contradictory beliefs in one's mind simultaneously, and accepting both of them.'[76] So, like self-deception, doublethink means sincerely believing in, and acting on, two contradictory statements. Orwell goes on to say that, in order for the sincerity of doublethink to be genuine, it must happen at both conscious and unconscious levels. This explains why there is no feeling of falsity or guilt when people doublethink. Unfortunately, Sartre cannot explain the mechanism of self-deception in this way, as he rejects as false the idea of the unconscious.[77]

The bottom line may be that Sartre has persuasively identified and explained an array of behaviour patterns which we recognise in others and ourselves. All of these behaviour patterns have one thing in common: they are our attempt to focus on one aspect of our being (our role, our past, our moral conscience, our personality) whilst denying other important aspects of our being (in particular our freedom).[78] Perhaps in the end we cannot construct a neat and tidy concept, such as 'bad faith', which explains these denials. Even Sartre seemed to believe this when, in *B & N*, he said, 'we can neither reject nor comprehend bad faith'.[79]

Sartre's concept of bad faith is complex. It tries to explain why, on the one hand, we must be aware of our freedom but, on the other, for most of the time we do not think of ourselves as free. But, as we have seen, there is also a moral dimension to Sartre's concept: the patterns of behaviour of bad faith are ones we ought to avoid. We should not deceive ourselves, we should not deny our freedom, we should not pretend that we are determined by our past, we should not try to become being-in-itself. So, what should we do? In *B & N*, Sartre does not really discuss the alternatives to bad faith,[80] but by the time of *E & H* he finds that he is able to offer an account of a more positive way of living. Let us now look at Sartre's views on how we should live and how we can avoid bad faith.

I **am** free

I'll talk and act as if I'm **not** free

Self-deception

Authenticity

... the actions of men of good faith have, as their ultimate significance, the quest of freedom itself. (E & H, p. 51)

The question we now face is how we should act if we are to avoid bad faith. Sartre rejects various possibilities, through having characters in his fiction act in many different ways, only some of which are authentic. Many of Sartre's characters choose to act in an immoral way, perhaps thinking that this is what freedom brings. But they are not really acting authentically, as they are simply reacting against an objective morality that does not exist. Some commit suicide to show how futile it is to live in a meaningless world – but, of course, this is a complete denial of freedom, since in death we are absolutely in-itself and lack all freedom. Others commit random actions (ACTES GRATUITS – *E & H*, p. 48), such as stabbing the palms of their hands in seedy cafés.[81] But Sartre condemns such motiveless or gratuitous acts: these people are simply avoiding the burden of responsibility that we all have to create meaning in the world – they are adding to its absurdity.

So, how should we act? Sartre tells us that we must avoid bad faith and must pursue its opposite, good faith or authenticity. People who act in good faith act in the full knowledge and recognition that they have absolute freedom. They make claims and take actions for which they know they hold responsibility. In other words, they lead authentic lives – authentic because they are not deceiving themselves that they have an essence or a determining role or personality; authentic because they not only realise this in an intellectual sense (as a philosopher who has studied Sartre might think 'I have absolute freedom') but also act on it. Remember, we can never define or renew ourselves with thoughts; it is only with action that we can give our lives meaning. This is what Sartre refers to as COMMITMENT: creating meaning through action. Sartre despises the sort of person who just sits around and talks; instead, we must act.

[Existentialism] declares that there is no reality except in action. It goes further, indeed, and adds, 'Man is nothing else but what he purposes, he exists only in so far as he realises himself, he is therefore nothing else but the sum of his actions, nothing else but what his life is.' (E & H, p. 41)

So, Sartre does offer guidance on how we should live. He says that, above all, bad faith must be avoided. We cannot blame our actions on our circumstances, on our emotions, on signs from God, on advice from other people, on our past or our upbringing or our society. Sartre tells us we should live authentically, and to do this we must:

■ be aware of our freedom
■ be committed to action
■ take responsibility for all that we do
■ be engaged in creating and inventing our lives.

We could describe Sartre's ethics, prior to *E & H*, as an ethics of authenticity, and these four goals as the values of authenticity. We shall see in Chapter 8 that we must add another two goals:

■ respect the freedom of others
■ take responsibility for others.

In the four examples below you are presented with a decision about how to act.

a) In pairs, work through each example in turn and discuss:

■ what you would do
■ why you would do it.

b) Ask yourselves whether your action is made in *good faith*, that is to say, is it *authentic*?

---

1 One day you are out walking in the countryside when you hear a booming voice and see a blazing light in the sky. The voice announces itself to be that of God. It tells you to go to your cousins' house and sacrifice their hamster to His greater glory. It explains where to find sleeping tablets so that your cousins will not know.

---

2 You are out walking in the countryside when you discover a large crack in the ground. Peering in, you discover a nice ring, which you try on. Immediately you discover that the ring has the power to make you invisible. You realise that with this ring on, you will be able to go into town and easily take whatever you like from any of the shops. Indeed, there is no limit to the things you could get away with.

---

3 You are a farmer and on the day of the harvest you notice some ominous storm clouds on the horizon. Realising that you will not be able to bring in the harvest before the crop is ruined by rain, you rush to your neighbour and ask for his help. You agree that you will help him next week in turn. The two of you successfully bring in the harvest. Next week, just as you are relaxing and watching TV, your neighbour comes knocking. He explains that a storm is brewing and that he needs help to bring in the harvest.

---

4 It is election day and the Elitist Party of Bad Faith are running a long way behind the People's Party for Authenticity in the polls. Although you support the PPA and believe that the election of the EPBF would be a disaster for the country and for many minority groups, you also recognise that there is no real chance of this happening. Your vote will make no difference either way to the election result. It is a long walk to the polling station in the next village and you are fed up of booming voices, magic rings and needy farmers.

Other people

We said on page 73 that an ethical theory is one that addresses the questions of how we should live and how we should treat others. We have seen that, in *E & H*, Sartre goes some way to answering the first question, in so far as he urges us to live an authentic life and to reject the impulse to run away from our freedom via bad faith. We shall now look at what Sartre's theory might have to say about the second question.

One of the biggest differences between *E & H* and *B & N* is in the account of how we treat other people. In *B & N*, Sartre devotes nearly a hundred pages to our relationships with other people, and most of it is doom and gloom: 'While I seek to enslave the Other, the Other seeks to enslave me . . . Conflict is the original meaning of [my relations with others].'[82] In contrast to this, *E & H* gives an incredibly positive account of our relationships with other people.[83] Let us look first at what Sartre has to say in *B & N* about other people.

As being-for-itself we are conscious of the world, and of the objects, artefacts and living things that furnish it. But it is not only objects that exist outside of ourselves. We are also conscious that we are not alone in the universe, that there are other self-conscious beings like us. What happens when the for-itself encounters another for-itself? What happens when we meet another person? True to the phenomenological method, Sartre tells a story to reveal what it is like to encounter other consciousnesses, other people.[84]

Imagine these two situations, then answer the questions at the end.

---

1 You are sitting on a bench in a park, there is no one in sight, and the whole world seems to revolve around you. You are aware of the nearby row of cypress tress, the fountain, the pattern of the path. You then hear something behind you and glance up. Someone is walking down the path towards you. They are staring at you. Now your experience of the world changes. (*How do you feel different, now that you are being looked at?*)

---

2 You are waiting for a friend outside their home, when you hear noises from the flat next door. You crouch down and peer in through the keyhole. You can vaguely see people moving about, but you cannot work out what they are doing. All of a sudden you hear heavy footsteps on the stairs behind you, and your whole world changes. (*In what way does your experience change, knowing that someone has caught you?*)

When confronted by objects, we negate them, in other words, we see them as *things* that we are not, things that can be controlled, things that have an essence. In Figure 7.1, the eye represents our consciousness; we are the centre of the world we experience – everything revolves around us.

■ **Figure 7.1**

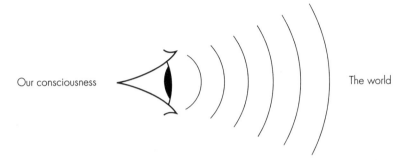

Our consciousness

The world

Sartre says that the same thing happens when we first encounter other people, or, as he often refers to them, THE OTHER. We see them as objects, as things which we can predict and control, in other words, as things which have an essence. But other people are not objects, they are self-conscious beings just like us, possessing absolute freedom, and they can escape any essence which we try to give them. So, as we become aware of other people, we become aware that there is a 'hole' in our world. There is a perspective upon the world which we ourselves cannot see. Sartre talks of another consciousness as a kind of drain-hole in our world (Figure 7.2).

■ **Figure 7.2**

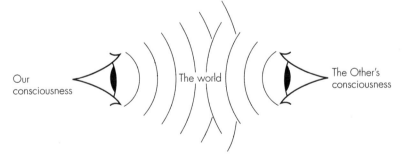

Our consciousness

The world

The Other's consciousness

So, there is a tension in our experience of other people: on the one hand, we treat them as objects but, on the other, we can feel their freedom – we can feel them treating us as objects. So, the Other constitutes a problem for us because, when we look at each other, we each try to OBJECTIFY the other person, to turn them into an object. Sartre calls this the struggle of 'THE LOOK' (in French: *le Regard*), as each person tries to possess the other's freedom without relinquishing their own. For example, someone walks into the burger bar where we are eating our lunch. We find amusing the way in which they walk, and the fact that their trousers are slightly too short. We pigeon-hole them as a 'Nerd', and start thinking of them only as a Nerd as they fumble foolishly for their change. Then they look at us. We suddenly become aware of the crumbs stuck around our mouth, of the slightly weird way in which we are sitting. We panic, as we think that this person is now seeing us as a Fool. We both look at each other, treating each other as an object and trying to possess the other's freedom, whilst doing our best to show that we are not an object, and that they are wrong to pigeon-hole us.

So, in *B & N*, our basic relationships with other people are negative ones of conflict, struggle and objectification. Sartre thinks that all relationships, even loving ones, boil down to a kind of battle between two people. Sartre gives countless examples of such relationships in his books and plays. In *No Exit*, the play about people trapped in hell, one of the characters concludes that 'hell is other people'.[85] The concepts of the object, of objectification and of the Other ring true to many people when describing relationships between people. Such concepts were used to great effect by Simone de Beauvoir in *The Second Sex*, to describe the way in which women are seen by men, and are now part of our common vocabulary.

► criticism ◄ The problem in *B & N* is that there seems to be no possibility of our having more positive relations with others; for example, we will never value them or respect their freedom. Yet Sartre himself had very close and fulfilling relationships with de Beauvoir and with his friend Paul Nazin, who was killed in the war. Most of us expect to experience a loving, reciprocal relationship with another person at some point in our lives, and many of us do. So, is Sartre not slightly overstating his case in *B & N*, and focusing only on the worst aspects of our relations with other people? By the time he came to give his lecture, *E & H*, Sartre himself had developed a more positive philosophical view of our relationships with other people.

Intersubjectivity

Sartre's lecture, *E & H*, offers for the first time in his philosophy an optimistic view of our possible relationships with other people. In the lecture he seems almost to have forgotten the depressing views of his earlier book, and he no longer claims that we try to possess other people's freedom. In fact he says the opposite, that we should respect and be committed to the freedom of others! This is because we live in a world of intersubjectivity:

The intimate discovery of myself is at the same time the revelation of the other as a freedom which confronts mine, and which cannot think or will without doing so either for or against me. Thus, at once, we find ourselves in a world which is, let us say, that of 'inter-subjectivity'. (E & H, p. 45)

What does Sartre mean by intersubjectivity?

more difficult

We saw in Chapter 4 that some philosophers, such as existentialists, reject as unattainable the idea of objectivity – of reaching an impersonal and true account of the world. Should we then conclude that all facts and truths are just personal, subjective opinions? Some philosophers have argued that there is a middle ground between objectivity, which is an impossibility, and subjectivity, which is a free-for-all. This middle ground is known as 'intersubjectivity' and it implies a connection or a common agreement between (inter-) two or more individuals (subjectivities).

I cannot obtain any truth whatsoever about myself, except through the mediation of another. (E & H, p. 45)

The philosophical concept of intersubjectivity is difficult enough to understand in the hands of the clearest writer. But, once again, this is one of those words that Sartre uses in his own special way. By intersubjectivity Sartre means something like 'the interdependency of subjectivity'. Subjectivity here refers to both our self-consciousness and our freedom. Interdependency means that our subjectivity depends on recognition by other people and at the same time their subjectivity depends on recognition by us. There are at least two possible interpretations of this concept:

- 'The other is indispensable to my existence, and equally so to any knowledge I can have of myself' (*E & H*, p. 45). Sartre could mean that we would not *know* about our subjectivity or our freedom without the existence of other people to recognise it in us. We would not be self-conscious without other people to make us self-conscious. Sartre could be saying that it is only when other people try to treat us as an object that we become aware of our freedom. Or, he could be saying that other people look at us and find that they cannot define us, our freedom escapes them, and so we then become aware of our freedom. Both of these interpretations are compatible with Sartre's views in *B & N* on our battle with other people.[86]

■ 'I am obliged to will the freedom of others at the same time as mine. I cannot make liberty my aim unless I make that of others equally my aim' (*E & H*, p. 52). Alternatively, Sartre could mean that we would not *value* our subjectivity or our freedom without the existence of other people to recognise its value. This interpretation goes beyond Sartre's account of other people in *B & N*, because it is saying that other people are essential for us to live a valuable and authentic life. We value our own freedom because other people value it, and without them we would not value it at all. And equally, because we have said that this is an interdependent relationship, we value the freedom of others, and this helps them to value it themselves.[87]

Why should we value the freedom of others?

This is one of the most important issues in *E & H*, and we shall devote a whole section to answering it in Chapter 8. However, we can give a quick answer to it here just from our knowledge of intersubjectivity. If we depend upon other people to value our freedom, then we value their freedom because it is only their freedom that makes it possible for us to value ours. This is a kind of 'you scratch my back and I'll scratch yours' relationship: we value their freedom because they value ours. Without this relationship no one would value freedom, and we would return to the depressing relations as described in *B & N*.

ACTIVITY   How do these two quotations conflict with each other?

We shall never place ourselves concretely on a plane of equality; that is, on the plane where the recognition of the Other's freedom would involve the Other's recognition of our freedom . . . Respect for the Other's freedom is an empty word. (B & N, pp. 408–9)

. . . in . . . willing freedom, we discover that it depends entirely upon the freedom of others and that the freedom of others depends upon our own. (E & H, pp. 51–2)

Reading the two quotations in the Activity on the previous page, we can see that Sartre's view in *B & N* on how we treat other people seems to contradict his view in *E & H*. In *B & N*, Sartre says that it is inevitable that we try to possess the freedom of other people, and, even if we want to, we cannot respect their freedom. In *E & H*, Sartre offers a very different view: that intersubjectivity means that we will the freedom of other people – we make their freedom part of our own project as a person of good faith, as someone who is authentic.

It is possible to resolve this contradiction by saying that Sartre had simply changed his mind in the years between *B & N* and *E & H*, or rather that his ideas had moved on. The bleak views of *B & N* are Sartre's description of the relationships between people who are in bad faith. But, in *E & H*, Sartre feels able to give an account of the relationships between people who have attained an authentic existence. In a relationship between people of good faith, mutual respect for each other's freedom becomes a real possibility.

Sartre's concept of intersubjectivity is hard to understand, because Sartre himself never clearly lays out what he is talking about. Sartre gets himself into these kind of difficulties in *E & H* because his personal values go beyond simply valuing the individual metaphysical freedom that he analysed in *B & N*. Sartre also values and respects other people and he thinks that we ought to as well. Political, social and moral freedoms are as high on his agenda as metaphysical freedom,[88] and he tried to incorporate this into his philosophy within *E & H*.

Key points: Chapter 7

What you need to know about the **ethical implications** of Sartre's theory:

1 Sartre never published a work of moral philosophy, but we can get an idea of his ethics from reading both *B & N* and *E & H*. In the former, he eventually suggests that the authentic actions of the individual are of value (see note 80 on page 134). In the latter, he tries to reconcile this individualism with his belief that we should value the freedom of others.

2 It is possible to draw out an existentialist ethic from *B & N*. Although Sartre does not see it as a work on ethics, he does address two important ethical issues: how we should live and how we should treat others.

3 Bad faith means deliberately acting as if we are not free. Sartre believes that we should avoid bad faith in all its forms, and he condemns those acting in bad faith. However, Sartre's condemnation is not, he says in *E & H*, a moral condemnation. Instead, it is a 'logical' judgement, which simply points out that those acting in bad faith are basing their choices on an error.

4 Authentic actions are those done in full knowledge of our freedom. Sartre proposes authenticity as the way in which we should live our lives. This means being fully committed to action and taking responsibility for it.

5 In *B & N*, Sartre's description of how we treat other people is very depressing. We treat them as if they were objects and as if they were not free. They also do the same to us, and so our relationships with other people are essentially ones of conflict.

6 In *E & H*, Sartre draws on the idea of intersubjectivity to give a more positive view of how we can treat other people. Intersubjectivity means the interdependence of subjectivities. In other words, we need other people to validate and value our own subjectivity and our own freedom; whilst at the same time they need us. This suggests that Sartre thinks that, even though we are all free to do what we want, we should respect the freedom of other people.

Ethical implications: Sartre's existentialist ethics

Introduction

Read E & H pages 24, 29–30, 50–3

We saw in the previous chapter how Sartre's existentialism might be taken as an ethics based on authenticity. It addresses two crucial moral questions: how should we live and how should we treat others? In answer to the first, Sartre promotes authenticity as the way of life for which we should be striving, and this means that we should shun bad faith in all its forms. In answer to the second, Sartre explains in some detail in *B & N* how we *do* treat other people, although it is only in *E & H* that he suggests how we *should* treat others. In *B & N*, Sartre describes how we are doomed to treat others as objects; in *E & H*, he hints at something more positive, namely our intersubjectivity, which means recognising and respecting the freedom of others. The question facing us in this chapter is whether Sartre can build a moral theory on the foundations of individual freedom.

It is in *E & H* that we find Sartre's most explicit public statement of what an existentialist morality might look like. The original title of Sartre's lecture already suggests this: *Existentialism is a humanism*. In other words, existentialism is not a theory which encourages anarchy or nihilism, as his critics suggest. Instead, it is a theory which sees humans as valuable in their own right. But Sartre's task of constructing an existentialist ethics is not going to be easy. Why is this?

- Because of his atheism, Sartre dismisses the view that there can be any objective moral values. So, an existentialist ethics cannot claim to be objective.
- Because of his condemnation of bad faith, Sartre believes that the individual must not follow, and is under no obligation to follow, moral rules (since to do so would be bad faith). So, an existentialist ethics must not issue prescriptive moral rules.
- Because of his belief in our absolute freedom, Sartre says that no one can tell us how to live our lives; we all must make our own choices. So, an existentialist ethics *must not* impinge on our freedom.

- Because of intersubjectivity, Sartre believes that we should respect the freedom of others. Yet to respect the freedom of others means that there are certain choices which none of us should take, for example, choosing to kill another person. So, an existentialist ethics will *have to* impinge on our freedom.

Finally, Sartre must try to combine the two most important values that he holds: the authenticity of the individual, and respect for the freedom of other individuals. We shall see later how successful this attempt to combine the rabid freedom of existentialism with a kind of socialist humanism actually was. We know that Sartre himself did not think that it was successful. In the late 1950s he turned to Marxism in order to have another go at constructing a coherent theory which respected both individual freedom and the fact that we have to live together in a concrete social world.

From the outline given by Sartre in *E & H* we have tried to reconstruct the arguments on which his ethical conclusions are based. The chapter is divided as follows:

- Sartre's rejection of conventional morality
- Sartre's first account of an existentialist morality
- Sartre's second account of an existentialist morality
- Problems with Sartre's existentialist morality
- Key points you need to know about Sartre's existentialist ethics.

Sartre's rejection of conventional morality

Sartre rejects conventional morality (which he calls the 'spirit of seriousness') on two counts:

- He believes that all conventional moral theories make a claim to objectivity, which is unjustifiable.
- He believes that people who follow conventional morality, and who feel obliged by the rules it lays down, are living in bad faith.

So, it seems as if an existentialist ethics is a contradiction in terms. Let us look at why Sartre rejects conventional morality.

An objective morality is impossible

Existentialism begins with subjectivity, because this is the only place we can begin. We cannot 'step outside' of our own individual perspective on the world and so objective knowledge in all human endeavours is an impossibility. In place of an analytical or scientific approach to the world, Sartre takes a phenomenological approach, beginning and ending with our own personal experiences of the world. So, even if there were a set of objective moral rules 'out there' in the universe, we would never know what they were, and so would never have to choose to obey them. In this sense, then, an objective morality is impossible: it cannot be known or grasped by individual subjectivity.

Sartre rejects an objective morality on other grounds too. Conventional moral theories claim to be universal, true across all times and places, and independent of human existence. This is what we mean when we say that they are objective. But Sartre believes that the only possible foundation of an objective, independent and universal morality is God, and God does not exist. Sartre recognises that some atheist philosophers have tried to construct an objective morality without God, but he thinks that they are mistaken. J.S. Mill's utilitarianism and Aristotle's virtue ethics are two famous examples of atheist and humanist moral philosophies;[89] but their theories, although persuasive, do not carry the same compulsion, the same obligation, as a moral law created by God.

The existentialist, on the contrary, finds it extremely embarrassing that God does not exist, for there disappears with Him all possibility of finding values in an intelligible heaven . . . It is nowhere written that 'the good' exists, that one must be honest or must not lie, since we are now upon the plane where there are only men. (E & H, p. 33)

For Sartre, if there is no God, then morality is merely a human creation, and in this respect it 'is comparable to the construction of a work of art' (*E & H*, p. 48). The artist is not given in advance any rules or values that they must follow, nor is there any predefined object that they must create. Instead, they invent the work as they go. According to Sartre, the absence of a God also means the absence of any rules, purpose or values, and so we are free to do anything we like. So, the same subjective invention and creation that takes place in art also takes place in morality. Existentialism is beginning to sound tempting for the creative thief or serial killer.

ACTIVITY   **1** Do you agree with Sartre that we create morality in the same way that an artist creates a painting?

2 Do you think that our judgements of a work of art as good/bad and of an action as good/bad have anything in common?

Sartre gives an example at the end of his lecture of two people who are in the position of inventing their moral values. The fictional characters whom Sartre draws on to illustrate his point are Maggie Tulliver (from the novel, *The Mill On The Floss*, by George Eliot) and La Sanseverina (from the novel, *The Charterhouse of Parma*, by Stendhal). Sartre imagines that both characters, faced with the same situation, would act differently. The dilemma in which he puts them is this: what to do about a man with whom they are passionately in love but who is already engaged to another woman? Maggie Tulliver would let her lover marry the woman to whom he is engaged; La Sanseverina would grasp her lover with both hands. Even though they are facing a similar moral dilemma, they choose opposite courses of action. But, although they choose differently, one person has not done something 'right' and the other person something 'wrong'. This is because they both act authentically by freely creating their different values. It is unfortunate that Sartre has chosen fictional characters in this example, as it means that we do not actually believe that they are free to choose anything at all! However, we can imagine real people facing the same decisions, and inventing their own values in their actions. The point is that moral values are created, there is nothing objective about them.

In *B & N*, Sartre also attacks the very feelings on which morality is based: our feelings of empathy for other people. As we saw in Chapter 7, when we encounter other people we feel threatened by them, and we cannot help treating them as an object. We see them as a menace to our freedom and we try to define them, to give them an essence. There seems to be no way in which such a suspicious approach to other people could provide any foundation for even a subjective, or intersubjective, moral theory.

This heady existentialist cocktail – of individual freedom, our separateness from other people, and the absence of any God-given objective morals – offers us, as Dostoyevsky said, a licence to do anything. We can kill, steal, lie and crib essays from the internet without breaking any moral law or code. At first sight, Sartre's existentialism seems to be fundamentally incompatible with any objective morality.

Belief in morality is bad faith

Sartre goes further than merely claiming that there is no objective morality. He actually condemns everyone who follows moral rules and principles by saying that such people are acting in bad faith.[90] Anyone who says 'I must do this' or 'I ought to do that' or 'I had to . . .' is denying their ultimate freedom to do anything they like. Obligations, feelings of conscience, social mores, duties, and commands: all of these are simply excuses which we seek out in order to avoid having to think and choose for ourselves. The most horrific examples of this are the excuses of the German soldiers and citizens who worked in the concentration camps. They maintained that they were following orders and had no choice in the matter, but Sartre's point is that they were choosing to follow orders and that the responsibility lies only with themselves.

I say that it is also a self-deception if I choose to declare that certain values are incumbent upon me; I am in contradiction with myself if I will these values and at the same time say that they impose themselves upon me. (E & H, p. 51)

▶ criticism ◀ Remember, there is a problem with Sartre's condemnation of self-deceivers. On the one hand, Sartre seems to be saying that we cannot make moral judgements because there is no objective morality. Yet, on the other hand, he seems to be making moral judgements by condemning people in bad faith and calling them cowards or scum. We mentioned on page 81 that Sartre gets around this by arguing that he is not making a moral judgement, but is making what he calls a logical judgement, or a 'judgement of truth'. Sartre is claiming that 'bad faith' is a descriptive, rather than a prescriptive, phrase. In other words (*E & H*, pp. 50–1), he is not saying that self-deceivers have done something morally wrong, only that they have made an error and are living according to a belief they know to be false. However, even though Sartre may say that he is making only a descriptive judgement, both his whole attitude to those in bad faith and his passion for authenticity suggest that he is, after all, making a value judgement.

The position Sartre takes on morality seems to be clear: we are lying to ourselves if we pretend that there are objective values which we must follow; values are invented by each of us individually; and our relationship with others is one of conflict and oppression. This position hardly provides strong grounds on which to demonstrate that existentialism is a humanism, or that an existentialist morality is possible. Indeed, the opening paragraphs of *E & H* show Sartre to be well aware that people saw existentialism as an amoral and anti-social theory. But Sartre does not really believe that 'everything (even murder) is permitted' within existentialism, and his goal in *E & H* is to show why this is not so.[91]

Read *E & H* pages 29–30

ACTIVITY   What do you think Sartre means by the following statements?

1 'The first effect of existentialism is that it puts every man in possession of himself as he is, and places the entire responsibility for his existence squarely upon his own shoulders.'
2 'To choose between this or that is at the same time to affirm the value of that which is chosen.'
3 'Nothing can be better for us unless it is better for all.'
4 'In fashioning myself I fashion man.'

From reading pages 29–30 in *E & H*, it seems as if Sartre is prepared to compromise his extreme individualism in order to make existentialism less abhorrent. In order to defend his theory against the attacks of his critics, he outlines two versions of what we might call an 'existentialist ethic'. We have identified the first account on page 29 of *E & H* and the second account on pages 51–2 of *E & H*. Both versions begin with the assumptions that there is no objective morality and that the individual is absolutely free. But Sartre also knows that he must create an existential ethics which does not refer to ideas of objective good and bad or to any other moral concepts that are a sign of bad faith.

Sartre's first account of an existentialist morality

Sartre's first account of an existential ethics occurs very early on in the lecture, just after the section on 'existence precedes essence'. This is a very dense part of the lecture, packed with ideas which roll over one another in an unhelpful way. We can only guess at how much of this part that Sartre's audience would have understood as they listened, since it is hard enough to follow when the text is in front of us to read.

When we say that man chooses himself, we do mean that every one of us must choose himself; but by that we also mean that in choosing for himself he chooses for all men . . . Our responsibility is thus much greater than we had supposed, for it concerns mankind as a whole. (E & H, p. 29)

The conclusion of Sartre's first account of an existential ethic is dramatic: he says that our choices are choices which we make for all of humanity. One way of helping us to understand Sartre's argument in this part of the lecture is to compare it to a very similar idea which can be found in Immanuel Kant's moral philosophy, the idea of UNIVERSALISABILITY.[92]

Both Kant and Sartre place freedom at the heart of their morality. Sartre believes that freedom lies in every decision we make. But Kant believes that freedom lies in our autonomy – in our decision to follow rationally determined rules and to be free from the emotions and desires that hold sway over our bodies.[93] In simple terms, Kant tells us that a moral action is one which has behind it a rule that is rational and reasonable to ask everyone to follow. It is unreasonable for us to behave in one way, let us say selfishly, and yet expect others to behave in another way, that is, selflessly. So, when we act, we should 'universalise' our moral rules; in other words, we should ask, 'what would the world be like if everyone followed this rule?' For example, if we were thinking about breaking a promise because it is inconvenient to keep it, we should consider what would happen if everyone followed the rule 'break promises whenever they are inconvenient'. We would realise that promises would be worth nothing. Kant concludes, therefore, that we should not break promises, or follow any other rules that cannot be reasonably followed by everyone.

Sartre does not go this far but he does pose a similar question to Kant: 'what would happen if everyone did this?' People who refuse to think about this are in bad faith because they are in denial about one of the consequences of our freedom, namely anguish (*E & H*, p. 30). Sartre even uses Kant's terminology ('legislator') when he says that someone making a choice is not only choosing for him/herself but 'is thereby at the same time a legislator deciding for the whole of mankind' (*E & H*, p. 30).

experimenting with ideas

Describe what would happen, or what the world would be like, if you universalised the following actions:

1 Joining the communist party
2 Getting married at the age of 35
3 Having three children
4 Obeying the voices in your head
5 Following orders to the letter in the army
6 Leaving home to fight for a cause in another country
7 Becoming a Catholic priest
8 Living in bad faith
9 Eating a chocolate éclair instead of a pastry slice
10 Deciding to be celibate for the rest of your life.

Sartre's conclusion that we must choose for everyone has a superficial similarity to Kant's idea of universalisability. Sartre appears to be saying that we should act in a way in which we would like other people to act. This is often termed the 'golden rule' of morality: treat others as you would wish to be treated. However, Sartre's argument is much more complex than this, and the implications go much further. On closer inspection we see that Sartre is not putting forward a straightforward Kantian system of ethics. He seems to be claiming that we *literally* choose for others, and that we are *literally* responsible for others. To understand this, we must put aside the simplified account and look at Sartre's argument in more detail: how does Sartre arrive at the idea that we must choose for all humanity?

To begin to answer this question, we need to unpick the dense and confusing argument contained in the passage on pages 29 and 30 of *E & H*. As you are probably aware by now, Sartre does not state his arguments in a rigorous and logical order. The Activity below should help you to make sense of Sartre's 'proof' that there is an existentialist morality.

ACTIVITY   **1** Each of the following statements is a simplification of one of Sartre's more complicated sentences from *E & H*. For each statement:

a) find the corresponding sentence in *E & H*
b) write down the exact words that Sartre uses in *E & H*.

Statement 1   There are no objective moral values (*top p. 24*).

Statement 2   I must accept responsibility for my choices (*top p. 29*).

Statement 3   Therefore a choice is a choice for everyone (*middle p. 29*).

Statement 4   Choices are identical with values (*bottom p. 32*).

Statement 5   A value is a value for everyone (*bottom p. 29*).

Statement 6   I must accept responsibility for everyone who makes the same choice as me (*bottom p. 29*).

2 Now (ideally with a partner) try rearranging these statements so that they form an argument, i.e. so that there are premises leading to a conclusion.

3 Discuss whether Sartre's argument is a good one. (Is it valid? Is it based on true premises? Does he use any hidden assumptions?)

Below we have tried to identify and evaluate the key premises in Sartre's argument (these are summarised in **bold**).

Premise 1 There are no objective moral values
Sartre's first assumption is that without a God there are no absolute or objective moral values. (*E & H*, p. 24)

► criticism ◄ For many atheist thinkers, this premise would be fairly uncontroversial (we looked at it in Chapter 6 when examining abandonment). But remember that many philosophers (such as Aristotle and Mill) would disagree and would claim that an objective morality is possible without God.

Premise 2 Choices are identical with values

Sartre then states that values exist only in the actions and choices that humans make. (*E & H*, p. 32)

This is also a reasonable premise, so long as we accept the first premise. We do seem to act in ways which we think are worthwhile. If we want to know what someone values, we need not listen to them preach, or read their works of moral philosophy. Instead, we need only follow them around for a couple of years, and we will soon find out what they really value by observing the things they choose to do. We have already looked at Sartre's idea, that we create our values in the same way that an artist constructs a painting – making individual, subjective choices about what is the right brush stroke, composition, subject matter. In a similar way we each make our own choices about the right thing to do. We invent and create morality, just as the artist invents and creates a work of art. For Sartre, values are choices and choices are values.

Sartre now goes on to analyse the very concept of 'value'. What does 'valuable' mean or imply?

Premise 3 A value is a value for everyone

On page 29 of *E & H*, Sartre states that nothing can be better for us unless it is better for all. In other words, things which we consider valuable or worthwhile are also things which we think other people should find valuable (e.g. marriage, p. 30).

ACTIVITY   Read through the actions listed in the Activity on page 98. Which of these actions would you say were 'better for all'? In other words, which do you think we should all choose to do?

Sartre seems to be saying here that all values, that is, end states that we wish to attain, are moral values, that is, end states that we think others should attain. This is why he conflates (as we have been doing in this book) values and moral values. The marriage example reveals the controversial nature of this assumption. People who think that marriage is good for them do not necessarily think that it is good for everyone, and we can think of any number of our own actions that we would not wish other people to imitate. Premise 3 is Sartre's problem premise, as it is an assumption that goes against our intuitions.

We might try to unpack this premise by drawing on other philosophers who have proposed similar ideas. Some have argued that part of the very concept of a 'good/valuable act' is a recommendation that other people should act in the same way.[94] For Kant, too, the idea of value was bound up in a universal law, something that bound everyone. Sartre, although he criticises Kant, is invoking Kant's principle of universalisability, which says that what is morally good for the individual is morally good for all individuals in similar circumstances.

► criticism ◄ Sartre provides no justification for this third premise, and it is difficult to agree with him. Does he think that the things valued by a teenager with a sweet tooth are things that a diabetic should value? Perhaps he might argue that values can be universalised only amongst individuals with the same needs, or in the same situation. Or perhaps he might say that only certain, significant or life-changing values should be ones we value for others. But, again, he does not expand on what he means and we are left speculating in his defence. In the absence of a better explanation, we must accept that Sartre does think that our own values are ones that we think should be held as valuable by everyone.

Premise 4 Therefore a choice is a choice for everyone
It appears as if this conclusion can be drawn from Premise 3 and Premise 2 above, and Sartre certainly seems to think so.

Sartre concludes from the first three premises that, when we choose, we choose for the whole of humanity. This goes much further than simply saying 'our values are values which we think that everyone should have'. On page 29 of *E & H*, Sartre implies that we are literally choosing for everyone else. We can apply this idea to all of the examples in Sartre's lecture. If Sartre's pupil chose to join the resistance, then he would have chosen it for everyone; if Abraham had killed his son, then he would have chosen this for everyone. But is it really true that, to use another of Sartre's examples, if we choose to get married, we are thereby committing every other human being to that choice? Sartre says yes; by getting married, we are committing others to the act of marriage whether we like it or not.

In other parts of *E & H* he makes the same point but in a less didactic way: we fashion ourselves and we fashion others (page 30); when we act we are making an image of a human as we would like a human to be (page 29); we act as though the whole of the human race had its eyes fixed upon us (page 32); we perform actions which are examples to everyone (page 32); we are condemned to invent humanity (page 34). The implication in these passages is not that we literally choose for others, but that we set an example to others through our actions. It is almost as if our choices were put on a pedestal for all to see and for some to imitate, and it is this for which we must take responsibility.

Either way, Sartre's conclusion remains: our actions and choices are done for not just ourselves but for everyone. Sartre goes on to draw out the full implications of this conclusion.

> **Premise 5 I must accept responsibility for my choices**
> We know from earlier in *E & H*, that if we are free, then we cannot blame our actions on others, or find excuses, our actions are ours alone.

Sartre can now reveal just how far our responsibility extends.

> **CONCLUSION**
> **I must accept responsibility for everyone who makes the same choice as me**

So, Sartre's final conclusion (on page 29 of *E & H*) is that we are responsible not only for our own actions but also for the whole of humanity's. In other words, when we act we must be aware that we are inviting others to act in the same way, and that we must bear responsibility if they choose to act in the same way. And so we can see how, in the passage on page 29, Sartre arrives at the 'golden rule', mentioned on page 99, that we should treat others as we should like to be treated.

Sartre's second account of an existentialist morality

... when once a man has seen that values depend upon himself ... he can will only one thing, and that is freedom as the foundation of all values ... I am obliged to will the liberty of others at the same time as mine. (E & H, *pp. 51–2*)

Towards the end of the lecture (on pages 51–2), Sartre outlines a further foundation for an existentialist morality. This second account specifically places freedom, rather than universalisability, at the heart of an existentialist ethics. In this version of his moral theory, Sartre goes further than merely saying 'when we act, we must consider other people'. He asserts that, when we will our own freedom, we must at the same time actively will the freedom of others. Before we look at the reasons why he says this we should first be clear about what Sartre means by 'will'. To will something means to try to bring something about, to 'forcefully choose it'. But we know that the things we choose, and the things we try to bring about, are, by his existentialist definition, our values. So, to will something means to value it. Therefore, when Sartre says that we must will the freedom of others, he means that we must value their freedom.

There is a problem, though, in reading this second account. Sartre, in his first sketch of his ethics, does make an effort to construct an argument, however confused it may be. But in the second version, there is barely a whiff of argument, just a series of assertions, leading to the claim that we should *will* the freedom of others. But why must we value the freedom of others as well as our own? Sartre hints at three possible reasons which support this conclusion, and he intertwines them in this part of the lecture. It is possible to unpick and reformulate these reasons, which we have done below.

Reason 1: Intersubjectivity

The first argument is one that can be found most easily in the text. It is connected to the concept of intersubjectivity that we analysed in Chapter 7.

> . . . *freedom is willed in community. We will freedom for freedom's sake, and in and through particular circumstances. And in thus willing freedom, we discover that it depends entirely upon the freedom of others and that the freedom of others depends upon our own.* (E & H, pp. 51–2)

Sartre makes it clear that our freedom does not occur in a vacuum; instead, the free choices we make, and our commitment to action, take place in particular concrete circumstances. Specifically we do not live in isolation from one another and so our freedom takes place in a community. This is where the idea of intersubjectivity comes in: our freedom is dependent on the freedom of others, just as their freedom is dependent on ours. It is dependent in the sense that we would not be aware of our freedom unless there were other people who were also free. Other people act as 'mirrors' for us, so that we are able to see their freedom and to see that we are like them. Other people also try to objectify us, but fail because our subjectivity escapes them. So, other people make us aware of our freedom. Moreover, because we live in communities which limit or restrict our actions, in this practical sense our freedom, or rather the range of choices available to us, depends upon other people.

So, our awareness of our freedom depends upon the existence of others, but so does the value we give to freedom. Values are a human creation, according to Sartre. If there were no humans, then there would be no values. We value our freedom only because other people – teachers, parents, governments, artists, journalists – talk about it as important, and act in order to protect it. We are all dependent upon each other to recognise and fight for freedom. We all will the freedom of one another.[95]

▶ criticism ◀ One of the main problems with this argument is that it slips from the metaphysical meaning of freedom to another meaning. Sartre recognises this when he says, 'Obviously, freedom as the definition of a man does not depend upon others' (*E & H*, p. 52). In other words, Sartre does not mean literally that other people make us free. We know that, for Sartre, what makes us free is the fact that we are being-for-itself and we have no essence: this is 'freedom as the definition of man'. Metaphysical freedom is a fact about us that cannot be given or taken away by other people. However, Sartre, when he talks about freedom being 'willed in a community', seems to be talking about another type of freedom: the range of choices we have within the laws and rules of a society. So, it may be true that we do 'will' other people's freedom in so far as we play a role in society, in shaping its rules, and in enabling their projects to take place. Similarly it may be true that our own projects, to write a book, or make a film or go to college, depend upon other people 'willing our freedom' and giving us the opportunity to do these things. But this argument does not demonstrate that we must will the metaphysical freedom of other people.

Reason 2: Authenticity

We have already seen the high value that Sartre places on authenticity: namely, living our life in full knowledge of the truth, and embracing this truth. What truths has Sartre demonstrated? That we are self-conscious, that we are free and that other people are self-conscious and other people are free. These truths seem undeniable, and to deny them would be bad faith. But merely acknowledging the fact that other people are free does not imply that we must *value* their freedom. So, why should we value their freedom as well as our own? This is how Sartre puts it:

Consequently, when I recognise, as entirely authentic, that man is a being whose existence precedes his essence, and that he is a free being who cannot, in any circumstances, but will his freedom, at the same time I realise that I cannot not will the freedom of others. (E & H, p. 52)

Sartre seems to be saying that, if we do not value the freedom of others, then we are moving away from authenticity into bad faith. Why is this so? To place a higher worth on our own freedom implies that we are intrinsically of more value than other people. But to believe in intrinsic values, in other words, values which exist independently of human creation, is bad faith: it is believing in *a priori* or objective morality. There is no reason we can find, within an existentialist position, to value our freedom but not everyone else's. So, to be consistent, and to be in good faith, we must value the freedom of others equally to our own.[96]

Authenticity thus underpins the argument based on intersubjectivity that we looked at above. In order to understand the dependence of our freedom on the freedom of others, we need first to have an authentic attitude to the world.[97] Only then will we see that we cannot value our freedom more than that of others, and only then will we start to consider the origins of our freedom in that of others.

▶ criticism ◀   Sartre is trying to demonstrate that we must value the freedom of others. The problem for the argument based on authenticity is that it seems to be saying that we should, in an ideal world, value the freedom of others. In his *Notebooks for an Ethics*, Sartre often talks about a state where everyone is authentic and everyone values the freedom of other people.[98] He refers to this new possible relationship with other people as 'generosity'. However, this is presented by Sartre as an *ideal* state, where everyone is authentic, rather than one that describes the world in which we live now. If Sartre's argument is that we must all be authentic, and part of authenticity means valuing the freedom of others, then he must show us why we are obliged to live authentic lives. If people choose to live in bad faith, then Sartre has no moral leverage which would force them to respect and value the freedom of others, and to attempt to force them would be an act of bad faith itself!

Reason 3: Universalising freedom

It is possible to provide a third argument to support Sartre's claim that we must value the freedom of others, although Sartre does not put forward such an argument himself.[99] The argument combines the idea of universalisability (proposed in *E & H*, p. 29) with the idea of the value of freedom (proposed in *E & H*, p. 51).

Premise 1 My choices depend upon my freedom

This is an uncontroversial premise. If we did not have freedom, if we were being-in-itself, then we would not have any real choice, we would be determined. Our capacity to choose depends upon our metaphysical freedom. Sartre goes on to say that a man comes to realise, 'that values depend upon himself...' (*E & H*, p. 51). In other words:

Premise 2 Choices are identical with values

We have seen above that, in the absence of any objective underpinning of value, our choices become our values. So, each of the following choices represents something we value: obeying an order; becoming a priest; eating an éclair; joining the resistance. Because our choices are our values and our choices depend on our freedom, we can conclude that:

Premise 3 My values depend upon my freedom

This follows from Premise 1 and Premise 2 and is what Sartre means when he says that 'Freedom [is] the foundation of all values' (*E & H*, p. 51). If we were not free, for example, if we were dead or were turned into stone, then we would no longer have any values. But, so long as we are free to make choices, then we are able to create values.

Premise 4 I value freedom because it underpins all my values

Sartre says: 'once a man has seen that values depend upon himself . . . he can will only one thing, and that is freedom as the foundation of all values' (*E & H*, p. 51). We know that to will something is to value it, so willing our freedom also means valuing our freedom.

Premise 5 My values are values for everyone

This premise is also taken from the previous account, and is simply Sartre's analysis of the concept of 'value'. If we think something is of worth, then we think it is of worth for everyone. The success of the argument turns on this premise, because if we recognise that freedom is of worth, then:

Conclusion: freedom is something I value for everyone

To put it in another way, when we decide to act, we are universalising not simply a particular choice but freedom itself. In summary, Sartre says that freedom underpins every choice we make, and so every value we invent. So, when we choose, we are not only choosing a particular action but also willing the freedom that enables us to make that choice. But Sartre also says that what we choose ourselves we also choose for everyone. Therefore, whenever we make any free choice of our own, we are also choosing freedom for the whole of humanity; we are universalising freedom.

▶ criticism ◀ The main problem with this argument lies with Premise 5, the universalisability premise. We saw in Sartre's first account of an existentialist ethics that we do not always want other people to value what we value. However, we also saw that we could refine this premise, by saying that we do want other people in the same situation as us to value what we value. So, we can defend Sartre against this criticism by saying that, with this version of the premise, all humans are in the same situation: we are all inescapably free, whoever we are.

With this global expression of the universalisability premise, the problems that occurred earlier do not arise. Sartre is no longer claiming that, when we choose marriage, we are thereby choosing (or recommending) marriage for everyone else. Instead, he is claiming that, when we choose marriage, we are actually choosing the freedom to get married for everyone else. This makes much more sense. Imagine that the government decided to ban marriage for all single people, and to make them live in single-sex monasteries. By doing this, the government would be disregarding our choice. Even if we were already married, and the law did not affect us, by getting married ourselves we would have already chosen the freedom for others to get married. And so married people should fight against a law that bans marriages.

So, there are three possible reasons why Sartre concludes that we must will, and thus value, the freedom of others:

- The first is based on the intersubjectivity of freedom: our freedom is dependent on the freedom of others and theirs is dependent on ours.
- The second is that authenticity demands that we place our freedom on an equal footing with everyone else's; to do otherwise would be bad faith.
- The third possible reason is that, when we act, we are choosing for everyone the freedom that underpins that act; we are universalising freedom.

We have now examined the two accounts of an existentialist morality that Sartre provides in *E & H*, both of which give us guidance on how we should live our lives. The early one concludes that we must take responsibility for the whole of humanity; the later one concludes that we must respect the freedom of other people. Let us return to the difficulties that Sartre faced in constructing an existentialist ethics, which we outlined in the introduction to this chapter:

- Both of Sartre's accounts of an existentialist ethics are based on our subjectivity, and both acknowledge that values are created by the individual through their actions. So, in that sense, his moral theory is not objective.
- Neither account gives us the opportunity to slip into bad faith, because neither prescribes any moral rules (unlike Kant's ethics). Instead, Sartre's existentialist ethics shows us how we can lead a truly authentic existence through understanding the full implications of our freedom.
- Both accounts place the freedom of the individual at their centre. The second account goes further, in that it posits freedom as the sole value we need to hold.
- The second account also argues that, by valuing our freedom, we thereby value everyone else's. So Sartre's moral theory does respect the freedom of others, and it impinges on our freedom only in so far as striving to live an authentic existence impinges on our freedom.

This lecture can be seen as the beginning of the 'radical conversion' that Sartre mentioned in *B & N*.[100] Sartre really does seem to have moved from a position of extreme individualism in *B & N* to a fledgling moral theory in *E & H*, a theory he explored further in his *Notebooks for an Ethics*. Some philosophers have referred to his moral theory as an 'ethics of authenticity',[101] because Sartre is advocating that we should act in an authentic way: we must recognise our own freedom in our actions; acknowledge that we are responsible for our actions; and choose freedom for others.

Problems with Sartre's existentialist ethics

▶ criticism ◀   Sartre seems to be using Kant's theory on the one hand, and rejecting it on the other. He ridicules any attempt at a 'secular morality' (*E & H*, p. 33), and he specifically rejects the work of Kant (*E & H*, pp. 27, 36, 49, 52). Yet, as we have seen, he does seem to draw on Kant in both versions of his existentialist ethics.

Sartre does acknowledge that both of their theories are grounded in freedom (*E & H*, p. 52), but also that there are crucial differences between their ideas on universalisability. Kant believes that it is rules that are universalised, and these become rules that humans are morally obliged to follow across all times and places. Sartre, unlike Kant, never says that we should universalise a rule, only that we should universalise an image or example: 'We think . . . that principles that are too abstract break down when we come to defining action' (*E & H*, p. 52). Sartre recognises that life is too unpredictable to say, for example, 'we must not break promises' for there may be circumstances when we must break a promise. Thinking that there are rules or principles which we are obliged to follow is a form of bad faith, and Sartre does not say that there are any rules that we ought to follow. We are free to imitate the actions of others or not; it is up to us.

▶ criticism ◀ How is it possible for one person to be responsible for another's actions (*E & H*, p. 30)? If each and every one of us is absolutely responsible for our own actions, then one cannot be responsible for another's actions, nor vice versa. Yet Sartre seems to say that one person is responsible for another's choices. Is he contradicting himself, or does he mean that responsibility is shared between the two? (If this is the case, then is he not again limiting our absolute freedom?) Whichever way we choose to interpret Sartre, it seems as if the absolute freedom of the individual that Sartre proposed in *B & N* is compromised or restricted by his efforts to make existentialism a viable theory of action, that is, one that will actually work in a community.

▶ criticism ◀ How is it possible for one person to choose another's actions (*E & H*, p. 29)? Can Sartre really mean this in a literal way?

Perhaps he is saying that one person metaphorically chooses another's actions, and that this means that, when we act, we are simply setting an example or precedent for others to follow. In other words, one person's actions put forward an ideal for how other people should behave (fashioning 'man'; *E & H*, p. 30). Or perhaps Sartre means that one person's actions influence another's, and give the latter a reason for copying the former; for example, when someone chooses to buy green products from the supermarket, they are 'choosing' for others because they are saying, 'Look at what I do – you should do the same.'

▶ criticism ◀ It is not true that what we value for ourselves we also value for everyone else. We have already seen on page 101 that someone with a sweet tooth would not want a diabetic to eat what they eat.

Sartre seems to acknowledge this problem at the beginning of the post-lecture discussion (*E & H*, p. 57). Here he agrees that, when choosing a chocolate éclair over a millefeuille (a kind of fancy pastry), a person is not choosing in anguish – in other words, they are not choosing chocolate éclairs for everyone. The problem is that Sartre gives us no criterion with which to distinguish significant or life-changing choices (such as marriage, which we apparently do choose for everyone) and insignificant ones, such as the éclair.

▶ criticism ◀ Sartre's moral theory seems to contradict his claim that there are no objective morals. Boldly asserting that 'freedom is the foundation of all values' certainly seems like an objective moral principle, and Sartre says that it is part of the universal human condition.

His defence could be that freedom is a subjective value which we all individually discover in ourselves when we embark on a phenomenological analysis of our being. In this way it can be universally known (amongst humans), without being objectively known.

▶ criticism ◀ *E & H* contradicts *B & N*. In *B & N*, Sartre claims that we wish to possess others' freedom, not respect it, whereas in *E & H* he says that we must respect it.

However, two years separated the lecture from the book, and Sartre's ideas had moved on. Sartre's notebooks indicate that he had begun to see his description in *B & N* of our relations with other people as a description of relationships between people in bad faith. In *E & H*, he is revealing his new idea that relationships between people living authentic lives are much more positive.

▶ criticism ◀ Finally, Sartre seems to be confusing two types of freedom. The kind of freedom that underpins all our choices and values is metaphysical freedom, freedom of will. But we cannot will metaphysical freedom for others, they simply have it as being-for-itself.

We can, however, will political freedom for others, and can fight to preserve their freedom in law. Sartre found it difficult to reconcile these two values (the metaphysical freedom of the individual and the political freedom of people in society) from within an existentialist framework. Sartre eventually rejected existentialism and developed his own theory of Marxism, a conversion more radical than anything existentialism could offer.

Key points: Chapter 8

What you need to know about Sartre's **existentialist ethics**:

1 An existentialist ethics is a moral theory which tells us how we should live and which gives reasons, supporting this conclusion, that are drawn from and are consistent with existentialism. *E & H* offers two versions of such a theory.

2 At first sight it appears that an existentialist ethics is a contradiction in terms. Sartre believes that objective moral values do not exist. He also believes that people who follow moral rules are living in bad faith. To be authentic we must invent our own values through our freely chosen actions.

3 Sartre's first attempt to outline an existentialist morality is based on the idea that what we value we value for everyone. Because values are essentially choices, Sartre concludes that what we choose we choose for everyone. Moreover, because choice brings responsibility, we are therefore responsible for everyone when we act.

4 Sartre's second sketch of an existentialist ethics tells us that we must value other people's freedom as well as our own. There are three possible reasons which support this conclusion:

  ■ The first is based on the intersubjectivity of freedom: that one person's freedom depends upon another's and vice versa.
  ■ The second reason is based on authenticity: if we value our freedom but do not value others', this suggests that we believe that we are intrinsically more valuable, but this is bad faith.
  ■ The third reason can be reconstructed by drawing on Sartre's first version of his existentialist ethics, which tells us that our choices are for everyone. Because freedom underpins all our choices, when we act we therefore choose freedom for everyone.

Sartre's defence of existentialism

Introduction

Read E & H pages 23–5, 42–7, 50–6

We have now looked in some detail at Sartre's theory and are in a position to return to the beginning of the lecture in order to assess the criticisms that Sartre says have been made against existentialism.

Many readers of Sartre's *Being and Nothingness* and of his novels and plays saw existentialism as a depressing and ugly theory which placed little value on human beings. The reason why Sartre gave his lecture in the first place was to defend existentialism against such attacks, and to show that it was, after all, a kind of humanism. There are at least four criticisms that Sartre outlines at the beginning of *E & H* and, taken together, they do amount to a serious attack on existentialism. If they are all true, then it is easy to see why people might say 'existentialism is not a humanism'. Having defended existentialism against these criticisms, Sartre is in a position to conclude that existentialism is, after all, a humanism.

The chapter is divided as follows:

- Criticisms of Sartre's existentialism
- Sartre's defence against these criticisms
- Sartre's conclusion: Existentialism is a humanism
- Key points you need to know about Sartre's defence of existentialism.

Criticisms of Sartre's existentialism

During the post-war months at the end of 1945, existentialism fast became the most important intellectual movement of the time.[102] Writers such as Albert Camus, Gabriel Marcel, Simone de Beauvoir, Maurice Merleau-Ponty and Sartre himself were establishing a body of existentialist literature which was read across the world. Sartre, already a leading literary figure at the beginning of the war in 1939, was world famous by the end of it. He was offered, and rejected, the Légion d'Honneur in 1945,[103] and he remarked of his popularity, 'It is not pleasant to be treated as a public monument during one's lifetime.'[104] There was already a backlash in some quarters against Sartre and his existentialist companions,[105] and Sartre began his lecture with a summary of the main criticisms that had been made against the theory.

Criticism A: Existentialism is pessimistic

First, it has been reproached as an invitation to people to dwell in the quietism of despair. (E & H, p. 23)

According to Sartre, existentialism stands accused of being a pessimistic philosophy: on the one hand, because it can lead to inaction and the 'quietism of despair' and, on the other, because it can lead to philosophical navel-gazing, without any real engagement in the world. In the third sentence of *E & H*, Sartre says that 'if every way to a solution is barred', then we start to see all actions as 'ineffective'. What could he mean by this? The solution to which he is referring may be an answer to a question that all humans face, namely, 'how should I live?' or 'what should I do?'

We have seen that Sartre rejects any external guides as to how we should live our lives: there is no God to provide a moral law; there is no human nature which can give us a clue as to what we should be doing; there is no ethical system to which we can turn for help; there are no rules or norms of society which can tell us how to behave. God, human nature, moral systems, social rules were once all potential 'solutions' to the question 'what should I do?' and yet each one of them has been rejected, or 'barred', by Sartre's existentialism. If Sartre is right, and we live in a world with no God, no purpose or direction, then one of the easiest things to do is to give up: to shrug our shoulders and think, 'what's the point of doing anything?' This would be a deeply pessimistic conclusion.

An equally pessimistic result of existentialism would be to decide that, rather than sit around and do nothing, we should try to find an answer through further philosophising. This kind of contemplation is a 'luxury' (*E & H*, p. 23) because only those rich enough not to have to work for a living could philosophise for any great length. This criticism comes from communist thinkers, and Sartre takes it very seriously.

Sartre wanted existentialism to change the lives of everyone in the world, he wanted his philosophy to be a philosophy of action. These goals would be completely undermined if this first criticism, that existentialism leads to the quietism of despair or to contemplation, were true.

Criticism B: Existentialism emphasises the uglier side of life

From another quarter we are reproached . . . for depicting what is mean, sordid or base. (E & H, p. 23)

According to Sartre's religious critics, existentialism over-emphasised the ugly and 'evil side' of life, whilst neglecting the more positive aspects of humanity.[106] Sartre even quotes a lady who, whenever she swore, said 'I believe I am becoming an existentialist' (*E & H*, p. 24). It is true that Sartre did write in a 'realistic' style about realistic people facing realistic situations. His stories are grounded in the bars and streets of Paris; his characters face real-life dilemmas – whether to have an abortion, whether to betray a friend, whether to lie, cheat or steal. (His collection of short stories, *The Wall and other stories*, gives a flavour of the ugliness to which these critics may be referring.)

This kind of realism in Sartre's writing may be seen as a progression from the nineteenth-century movement amongst painters and writers known as 'naturalism'. Sartre refers to this movement, and to one of its key figures, Zola, on page 24 of *E & H*. But it is not just in his novels and plays that Sartre can be said to be guilty of emphasising the worst aspects of human existence. Some of his most misanthropic views can be found in *B & N*, where Sartre outlines at length the more depressing aspects of our relationships with others: objectification, sadism and masochism.

Criticism C: Existentialism isolates the individual

. . . we are also reproached for leaving out of account the solidarity of mankind and considering man in isolation. (E & H, p. 23)

This is a serious criticism made by communists against Sartre, and it is serious enough to be taken up again at the end of the book in the discussion between M. Naville and Sartre. Existentialism begins with subjectivity, with the individual's freedom and their encounter with the world. A Marxist or communist would see this as a bourgeois philosophy, because it stems from the privileged middle classes who do not have to do any serious work for a living, but who live sheltered lives, and who believe that it is up to individuals to look after themselves.

Even more damning than this, communists see all bourgeois philosophy as part of an ideology whose purpose is to maintain existing power structures, with the middle classes exploiting the working classes. The working classes will not become aware that they are being exploited so long as they see themselves as individuals, and remain unaware that they are a member of a vast class of people who are all in the same impoverished position. So, the bourgeoisie, if they are to maintain their power, have a vested interest in making sure that people never develop a 'class consciousness'. Existentialism, with its focus on individual freedom, helps to ensure that the middle classes maintain their power. It does this by encouraging people to consider themselves as individuals, in isolation from other people, and never as members of a wider socio-economic class.[107]

Criticism D: Existentialism is an amoral theory

Everyone can do what he likes, and will be incapable . . . of condemning either the point of view or the action of anyone else. (E & H, p. 24)
People say to us, 'Then it does not matter what you do'.
(E & H, p. 47)

Sartre first mentions this criticism at the beginning of the lecture, but he comes back to it later in more detail, and he divides it into three separate accusations.

[D1] *First they tax us with anarchy. (E & H, p. 47)*

Many critics said that existentialism recognised no form of morality and encouraged people to behave amorally (without any morals). Much of the evidence for this comes from Sartre's fiction, as his characters certainly behave without regard or concern for the normal conventions of moral behaviour. It would seem that Sartre believed that if there is no God, then there is no moral law, or any form of objective morality. At first sight, then, it seems as if existentialism encourages individuals to act in whatever manner they please, without any fear that what they are doing is wrong, because for an existentialist 'wrong' has no meaning.

[D2] *. . . then they say, 'You cannot judge others, for there is no reason for preferring one purpose to another.'*
(E & H, p. 47)

There is a further consequence of Sartre's rejection of objective morality, and the critics attack him for this as well. It is that moral judgements no longer become possible and therefore presumably moral arguments and discussions are meaningless. This is the attack that Sartre takes most seriously, because he feels deeply that existentialism is a moral theory.

[D3] *Finally, they may say, 'Everything being merely voluntary in this choice of yours, you give away with one hand what you pretend to gain with the other'.*
(E & H, *pp. 47–8*)

We mentioned on page 81 the problem that someone might deliberately choose to act in bad faith. Sartre's critics are saying that, if his theory does not make any moral prescriptions, telling us how we should behave, then he is opening the door for people to use their freedom to act in bad faith.

ACTIVITY Given what you already know about Sartre, how do you think he might respond to criticisms **a–d**? What parts of his theory do you think he could draw on to rebut these attacks?

Write down Sartre's response to each of the following accusations:

a) Existentialism encourages inaction.
b) Existentialism emphasises the uglier sides of life.
c) Existentialism focuses only on the isolated individual.
d) Existentialism is an amoral theory because:

- it encourages anarachy
- it cannot judge people
- it allows people to choose bad faith.

Sartre's defence against these criticisms

Sartre builds up his defence throughout the whole lecture. Although he is interested in explaining his theory of existentialism to the audience, he is much more concerned with demonstrating that existentialism is not the threatening philosophy that the popular French press had made it out to be.[108] We can see the defence mount up throughout *E & H*, until Sartre feels able, finally, to conclude that existentialism is a humanism. Let us take each of the criticisms in turn and look at Sartre's defence.

Defence against criticism A: Existentialism is optimistic

> ... the existentialist says that the coward makes himself
> cowardly, the hero makes himself heroic. (E & H, p. 43)

The criticism made against Sartre was that existentialism is
pessimistic because it encourages us to give up on life, and
either do nothing or retreat into irrelevant philosophical
contemplation. This criticism is specifically addressed by
Sartre on pages 42–4 of *E & H*. Here Sartre emphasises the
optimism inherent in existentialism and the way in which
existentialism is committed to action.

It is optimistic because it explicitly rejects the apathy of
quietism as a valid attitude to life. Far from leading to
inaction, existentialism leads to action as it encourages us to
realise our freedom. Existentialism is the only theory that
does not treat humans as if they were objects, with a fixed
human nature. Instead, it treats humans with the dignity they
deserve, by acknowledging and respecting their freedom. It is
also optimistic because it says that each and every one of us is
free to choose our own life through our actions. It does not
believe that there is some 'fate' awaiting us all, or some force
of nature pushing us forward – that would be pessimistic.
Sartre attacks the novelist Emile Zola for describing his
characters in this way. Instead, existentialism asserts that we
create our own future and can invent ourselves through our
actions: we can become either a coward or a hero, it is up to
us. Far from being pessimistic, existentialism is an invigorating
and empowering theory and one of the most optimistic
theories ever written.

Defence against criticism B: Existentialism is not as depressing as conventional wisdom

> ... what could be more disillusioned than such sayings as
> 'Charity begins at home' or 'Promote a rogue and he'll sue
> you for damage, knock him down and he'll do you homage'?
> (E & H, pp. 24–5)

The criticism was that existentialism emphasises the ugly and
depressing side of life, and neglects joyful things such as the
smile of a baby. Sartre does not take this too seriously and,
unlike his other defences, he deals with it right at the
beginning of his lecture (*E & H*, pp. 24–5). He argues that
existentialist writing is no more ugly or evil than any other
realistic or 'naturalistic' novels, such as those by the

nineteenth-century novelist Emile Zola. He seems to be suggesting here that people always respond in an outraged fashion to contemporary novelists who give a realistic description of the world. But since no one was still horrified by Zola's work, presumably, given time, Sartre's work too would lose its shock value.[109]

The second part of Sartre's defence turns on a comparison between the advice given by existentialism and the advice given by 'common sayings' on how we should live our lives. People who condemn existentialism for its bleak view of life are often those who believe in old sayings which encourage us to be selfish, or to keep in our place, or never to try anything new (*E & H*, pp. 24–5). Sartre says that, compared with depressing conventional wisdom like this, existentialism is actually really positive, with its emphasis on the possibilities that freedom brings to all of us.

Defence against criticism C: Existentialism unites individuals

Thus the man who discovers himself directly in the cogito *also discovers all the others.* (E & H, p. 45)

The criticism faced by Sartre from his communist opponents was that his theory begins and ends with the individual, with no attempt to encourage individuals to regain solidarity with each other. Sartre deals with this on pages 44–7 of *E & H*.

It is true that existentialism begins with subjectivity, with Descartes' *cogito*, and hence might appear to treat the individual and not the community as of primary importance. The reason, however, why Sartre says that we must begin here is not because of his bourgeois values and ideology, but because, according to him, all philosophy must begin with a sure foundation, a point of certainty. The one truth that we can find is that we are self-conscious beings and so existentialism must begin with individual subjectivity and must investigate it fully.

But subjectivity is not the full story. According to Sartre, we come to realise that we are dependent on other individuals, and they are dependent on us, both for our self-consciousness and for our freedom. This intertwining of subjectivities, which we have seen Sartre refer to as intersubjectivity, means that existentialism does not consider only the individual in isolation. We act in a world full of free subjects like ourselves, and, as we act, we must consider and respect their freedom.

There is another aspect of Sartre's theory which brings individuals together, the human condition. Although Sartre acknowledges that there is no human nature which we all have in common, there is a 'universality of *condition*' (*E & H*, p. 46). What Sartre means by the human condition is not some mysterious essence, but the fundamental situation in which we all find ourselves. This situation which we all share consists of two things: our freedom, which we all encounter and deal with ourselves, and our facticity, which is the backdrop to our individual freedom against which we act. This facticity clearly differs from person to person, but each of us faces our limitations and strives to achieve our goals within our limitations. Thus, humans across different times and places can all understand one another's goals, because we are all living within the same human condition.

Defence against criticism D: Existentialism is a moral theory

The final criticism was that Sartre's theory has no moral leverage. Sartre divided this into three separate attacks:

- Existentialism rejects moral values.
- Existentialism cannot judge the moral actions or beliefs of other people.
- Because it is not prescriptive, existentialism actually makes bad faith a possible choice for people!

We shall look at Sartre's defence against each of these criticisms in turn.

[D1] ... *once a man has seen that values depend upon himself ... he can will only one thing, and that is freedom as the foundation of all values.* (E & H, p. 51)

The accusation is that Sartre's theory leads to anarchy and it does not matter what we do. But we have seen that, for Sartre, it absolutely does matter what we do. We must not act in bad faith (see D2 overleaf), but must try to live an authentic existence, in which we act in full awareness of our freedom. We cannot simply act randomly, as André Gide encourages us to do (*E & H*, p. 48), because by acting in this manner we are simply adding to the meaninglessness of the world, and are refusing to accept responsibility.[110] Nor must we act as if our actions had no effect on others. Sartre outlines a moral theory which tells us that we must accept responsibility for the whole of humanity and that we must respect the freedom of others.

It is true that there is no objective morality, and so the existentialist realises that we must construct our own values. No God exists to create objective values; the only values that do exist are those created by us through our choices. The only authentic morality is one in which we acknowledge that our choices are made not just for ourselves, but for everyone.

[D2] *I reply that it is not for me to judge him morally, but I define his self-deception as an error. (E & H, p. 51)*

Sartre was criticised because, in doing away with objective morality, he was seen also to do away with the possibility of any meaningful judgement of people's behaviour and choice of life. Sartre, however, does consistently make judgements, in particular of the cowards and scum, and of all the rest of us who act in bad faith. He maintains that he is able to do this by claiming that his judgement is not a moral judgement, but a judgement of fact (*E & H*, p. 51). We can judge self-deceivers just as we can judge anyone who has made a mistake; their mistake is just a bigger one, they are living a lie by pretending that they are not free and are not responsible for their actions. Sartre says that he can make a moral judgement, which is that freedom takes the central position in our new understanding of morality (*E & H*, p. 51).

[D3] *There is no reason why you should not [choose bad faith], but . . . the attitude of strict consistency alone is that of good faith. (E & H, p. 51)*

Sartre seems to be admitting here that existentialism has no response to someone who chooses to be in bad faith, except to say 'you are being inconsistent'. This is actually quite a damning thing to say, as very few people can deliberately hold two inconsistent beliefs. It is foolish to say, 'I know that the Earth is round, but I'm going to pretend that it's not'; or 'I know that there's no God, but I'm going to pretend that there is.' People do not consciously hold inconsistent beliefs, because as soon as their attention is drawn to the inconsistency they tend to reject one or other of the beliefs as false. Someone who has recognised their absolute freedom, but who chooses bad faith, is saying, 'I know that I'm free but I'm going to pretend that I'm not.' For Sartre, choosing bad faith is foolish, dishonest and inauthentic: it is the attitude of the cowards and the scum.

So, Sartre's critics are wrong, at least according to Sartre. He hopes to have shown that it is not existentialism that has worrying consequences for morality, but the 'spirit of seriousness' that characterises all other moral theories. Existentialism encourages responsibility, not a denial of responsibility; it encourages action, not the quietism of despair; and it encourages respect for the freedom of others. Existentialism sees values as created by us, not given as part of the fabric of the world, and they are all the more valuable for that. Morality cannot be taken for granted, it is something we must create and for which we must take responsibility.

By the end of the lecture, Sartre feels that he has defended his theory against all of the criticisms aimed at him. But the success of his defence depends upon the strength of the arguments he has given to show that we are free, that we invent values and that we must value the freedom of others. If these arguments are flawed – and we have offered many criticisms of them – then his defence may not have been as successful as he thought.

Sartre's conclusion:

Existentialism is a humanism

This is humanism, because we remind man that there is no legislator but himself; that he himself . . . must decide for himself; also because we show that . . . always by seeking, beyond himself, an aim which is one of liberation or of some particular realisation, that man can realise himself as truly human. (E & H, pp. 55–6)

In the closing paragraphs of the lecture, Sartre gives an impassioned summary of existentialism and its claim to be a humanism. Remember that humanism, in its moral sense, can be said to propose either, or both, of the following beliefs:

- Humans are valuable.
- Values and morality have their source in humanity.

To these, existentialist humanism adds a third belief:

- The value we give to humans must be an authentic value.

The types of humanism mentioned above hold the first two beliefs to be true, but they are not authentic. It is only existentialist humanism that values humans whilst avoiding bad faith. So Sartre, before he outlines his own humanism, takes care to distinguish existential humanism from other kinds of humanism.

Sartre acknowledges that it is rather strange that he is advocating existentialism as a humanism. After all, in his novel *Nausea*, Sartre's attitude to humanism is quite vicious. When

Roquentin, the protagonist, is confronted by a humanist proclaiming a love for humanity he thinks: 'People. You must love people. People are admirable. I feel like vomiting.'[111] Sartre ridicules humanists for their 'blindness', their tendency to lump everyone together without ever noticing that people are individuals. So, the humanism that Sartre is portraying in *E & H* is certainly not the kind of humanism that thoughtlessly values human beings.

In *E & H*, Sartre gives a further example of the kind of humanism he rejects. He quotes from a book by Jean Cocteau,[112] in which a character, whilst flying over mountains, declares that 'Man is magnificent!' (*E & H*, p. 54). Clearly this character is overwhelmed by the scale of human achievement, by its triumph over the constraints of nature in inventing aeroplanes. But Cocteau's character believes that we can all share in the achievements of only a few, simply because we are human beings: all humans are magnificent. For Sartre, this kind of humanism has dangerous consequences. On the one hand, it can lead to bad faith, because it encourages us to think of ourselves as having an essence, that is, certain characteristics which we share with all other humans. On the other hand, it can lead us to think of all humans as inherently valuable or good. Sartre refers to this as the 'the cult of humanity' (*E & H*, p. 55). The idea of a cult implies the idea of both worshipping and mindless obedience. Such a belief is a dangerous kind of humanism as it can result, in Sartre's eyes, in fascism. This may seem like an extreme thing to say, but Sartre had witnessed how, in Germany, the cult of humanity had led to the fascism of the Nazis.[113] For Sartre, the notion of the fixed value of humanity is a false idea which robs us of our freedom to reassess, to re-evaluate ourselves afresh in every new situation.

Existentialism as a humanism

Therefore, you can see that there is a possibility of creating a human community. (E & H, p. 54)

Let us now look at the climax of the lecture: Sartre's declaration that existentialism is a humanism. Two questions remain for us: how has Sartre arrived at his conclusion that existentialism is a humanism, and what type of humanism is existentialism?

We said on page 121 that humanism means both valuing humanity and placing the source of value in humanity. Has Sartre done enough in his lecture to show that existentialism meets these criteria? Let us take each in turn.

■ Existentialism values humanity

This is because:

- It is the only theory which does not make human beings into objects, but preserves their dignity (*E & H*, p. 45). Unlike other theories, existentialism begins with subjectivity, it recognises individuals as absolutely free, and it rejects the view that humans are predetermined.
- It goes beyond individuals valuing their own freedom. Sartre's existentialist morality demands that we value the freedom of all human beings, not just our own (*E & H*, p. 51).
- It is incredibly optimistic about what individuals can achieve through their action. Whilst it recognises the limits of our facticity (see page 54), it still encourages us to act, and to change our lives through our own projects (*E & H*, p. 28). We can go beyond what we have done in the past; we are, in Sartre's term, self-surpassing (*E & H*, p. 55).
- It is not a philosophy which patronises humans by saying that we are not responsible for our actions. Instead, it shows a deep respect for humans by placing responsibility firmly on our shoulders (*E & H*, p. 29).
- It makes the values we hold – which are not forced upon us, or given to us, but freely chosen by us – more valuable. This is because the source of value lies in humanity, not in some external moral law.

■ Existentialism places the source of value in humanity

This is because:

- Moral values must be created somewhere, but there is no God to have created them (*E & H*, p. 34).
- If there is no God, then there is no possibility of finding any *a priori* source of morality. This means that, contrary to the beliefs of other atheistic philosophers, there are no objective moral rules or values which can be discovered (*E & H*, p. 33).
- If God did not create values, then humans must be the source of their creation. Each of us creates our own values through the choices we make (*E & H*, p. 54). As Sartre says at the end of the lecture, man has 'no legislator but himself' (*E & H*, p. 56).
- Even if there were a God, this would make no difference to existentialism. We still have to find value for ourselves (*E & H*, p. 56).

ACTIVITY In order to conclude that existentialism is a humanism, Sartre can pull on the threads that he has woven throughout the lecture. For each of the following themes, write down how, directly or indirectly, it contributes to Sartre's conclusion that existentialism:

a) values human beings
b) places the source of values in human beings.

1 Existence precedes essence
2 Atheism
3 Subjectivity
4 Freedom
5 Anguish
6 Responsibility
7 Abandonment
8 Despair
9 Rejection of quietism
10 The optimism of existentialism
11 The morality of existentialism.

The ideas mentioned in the Activity add up to the view that existentialism is a theory which values human beings and places the origin of values in human beings. So, existentialism is a humanism in so far as it meets the two criteria outlined above. But what kind of humanism is it? We have seen that Sartre is at pains to distinguish it from other forms of humanism. But what makes existentialist humanism so different? We can add a third criterion, an existentialist criterion, to the other two:

■ Existentialist humanism is an authentic humanism

Sartre's concluding remarks in the lecture reveal not only the passion he feels for his existentialism but also the incredibly optimistic view he takes of human beings. Here Sartre is saying that the value that existentialists place in us is very different from the value other humanists place in us. We have seen that other humanists may regard us as innately good, but Sartre cannot abide this view as it is a form of bad faith. We are free, and are not 'innately' anything at all. We can transcend both our past and our present circumstances by reinventing ourselves and it is this capacity for transcendence that makes us valuable. We are what we make of ourselves, and so long as we are alive our future is undetermined and is full of possibilities. As Sartre says, 'Man is still to be determined' (*E & H*, p. 56).

The value that the existentialist places in humanity is the value of their potential, the value of their possibilities, the value of their freedom. This, for Sartre, is an authentic humanism, and this enables him to say, finally, that existentialism is a humanism.

Key points: Chapter 9

What you need to know about Sartre's **defence of existentialism**:

1 At the beginning of his lecture, Sartre outlines four main criticisms laid against his existentialist theory:

- It is pessimistic.
- It focuses only on the depressing aspects of life.
- It considers the individual in isolation from others.
- It is, in at least three respects, an amoral theory.

2 In the last third of the lecture, Sartre turns to his defence of existentialism against these criticisms:

- It is optimistic because it sees us as free and encourages us to act on this freedom.
- It is certainly not as depressing as the platitudes most people offer.
- It sees individuals as bound up with one another through intersubjectivity.
- It is a moral theory, and is able to make judgements and to offer good reasons for living an authentic existence and for valuing other people.

3 Finally, Sartre is in a position to make his conclusion: that existentialism is a humanism. It is not the sort of humanism that sees people as innately good or valuable. However, it does value people and it does make us the source of value. Existentialism is an authentic type of humanism because it values our potential and our freedom rather than some inner essence.

Glossary

This picks out some of the terminology used by Sartre in *Existentialism and Humanism*, together with some of his most important concepts from *Being and Nothingness*. When reading *E & H*, you may find it helpful to have the glossary at hand in order to make Sartre's ideas clearer.

A priori   A Latin term which usually describes a belief (or knowledge) that is known prior to or independent from experience. For example '1,000,000 + 1 = 1,000,001' can be known independently of counting a million and one apples. Sartre uses the term when he is talking about the possibility of values or moral laws that are **objective** and independent from human beings.

Abandonment   The second of the three emotions analysed in *E & H*. Sartre uses abandonment to refer to our realisation that God does not exist, and to the accompanying deep feelings of loss. These feelings of loss encompass the loss of purpose to our lives, the loss of **objective moral** values and the loss of any human nature or **essence** that may guide us through life. Because we are abandoned it is up to us to find our own way in life, and to create our moral values as we go. Sartre must be using the word 'abandonment' in a metaphorical way, as he does not literally believe that there once was a God, who has now vanished. Rather, humans once believed that God exists and now believe he does not.

Acte gratuit   Many of the characters in Sartre's fiction engage in sudden and random actions. *Acte gratuit* is a phrase used by the French novelist André Gide to describe any action done without a rational foundation or motive. Sartre says that such actions cannot be valid **authentic** choices, even though they are supposedly 'free'. This is because committing such random actions is simply a way of trying to avoid the awful responsibility we must bear.

Anguish   The first of the three emotions analysed in *E & H*. For many existentialists, including Sartre, anguish is our basic emotional response to **freedom**. The realisation that we are free, that there is no path we must follow, no destiny written down for us, and no one who can help us, leads to an immense feeling of unease and anxiety about our life. In *E & H* Sartre ties these horrible feelings of disquiet to the responsibility that freedom brings (something we all hate) and in particular to the responsibility we must bear for the whole of humanity when we act. Existentialist anguish is often called 'angst'.

Angst   See **anguish**.

Atheism   The belief that God does not exist. In Western philosophy this usually refers to the non-existence of God as described in the Judeao-Christian tradition. Atheism is one of the foundations Sartre gives for his theory in *E & H*. However, at the end of the lecture Sartre admits that proofs of God's existence or non-existence are irrelevant to the existentialist claim that we are free and must create our lives for ourselves.

Authentic/authenticity   Authenticity is the very opposite of **bad faith**. Someone who is authentic is someone who lives their life in the full awareness that they are **free**, that they are responsible for their own actions and they are responsible for the actions of others. For Sartre, this is (or should be) the ultimate goal of all humans, and for this reason it lies at the heart of Sartre's existentialist morality.

Bad faith   Bad faith (in contrast to **authenticity**) is the attempt that we all make to deny the truth of our absolute **freedom** and absolute responsibility. In *E & H* it is referred to as 'self-deception', because we are deliberately deceiving ourselves about our freedom. If we are **cowards** there are lots of tricks we can use to avoid facing up to our freedom, and all of these tricks constitute bad faith: for example, pretending we have a fixed personality; blaming the advice we have been given; pretending we are biologically or socially determined; taking on roles that we think limit our choices; pretending there is an **objective moral** code that we must follow. In *E & H* Sartre says he is not making a moral judgement by saying people are in 'bad' faith. Instead, he claims he is pointing out the error of their ways, they are in 'mistaken' faith.

Being-for-itself   Also referred to as 'the for-itself'. This is one of two types of being in the world described by Sartre in *Being and Nothingness*. In basic terms, Sartre thinks only of humans as being-for-itself. It is a form of **existence** that is **self-conscious**, capable of reflecting on itself as well as on the world. It is also a form of **existence** that is capable of negating the past, and imagining different possible futures. Because of this gap between its past and its future (which Sartre thinks of as **nothingness**), being-for-itself is absolutely **free**. Sartre does not mention the for-itself in *E & H*, but it is a fundamental concept within his existentialist philosophy.

Being-in-itself   Along with **being-for-itself** this is one of the two types of being Sartre identifies in *B & N*. According to Sartre, anything that is not self-conscious is being-in-itself. So, both natural and artificial objects, such as stones and paper-knives, are being-in-itself. These objects do not possess any **subjectivity** and they are **determined** by what they are (for example, their biology or the purpose they have been made for – their **essence**).

Cogito, **the**   Shorthand for Descartes' conclusion, '*cogito ergo sum*': 'I am thinking therefore I exist' – I may be able to doubt everything else, but I cannot doubt that I am thinking and that I am aware of my own existence. For Sartre, the *cogito* is the only possible basis for philosophy, meaning that we must begin philosophy with the fact that we are individual, **self-conscious** beings. Sartre connects the *cogito* to **subjectivity** as the starting point of existentialism.

Commitment   Also referred to as 'engagement'. For Sartre, commitment is the attitude to life and action of someone who is **authentic**. It means engaging in the world through action (avoiding **quietism**) in the full knowledge that we are free and responsible; and in the full knowledge that there is no meaning or purpose to our lives except the one we create through our actions.

Communism   This was one of the most important political movements of the twentieth century. It refers to any social system where property is not private, but is commonly owned by everyone. For followers of the German philosopher, Karl Marx, communism referred to the future society which, once capitalism had been overthrown, would be classless and truly democratic. For many intellectuals this was a compelling idea and one they had either to embrace or to reject. Sartre, in the period of *E & H*, felt that he needed to defend his ideas against communists, who attacked existentialism because it was a bourgeois luxury and because it encouraged individual action rather than class struggle.

Cowards   In *E & H* Sartre calls people who hide from or deny their absolute **freedom** 'cowards'. This is a specific sort of fear of freedom and should not be confused with ordinary cowards, whom Sartre also talks about in *E & H*. People who are cowards in the special sense are self-deceivers and are acting in **bad faith**. Sartre may have used such a derogatory term to try to shock us into considering whether we are running away from our freedom.

Despair   The third of the emotions discussed in some detail in *E & H*. For Sartre, despair is the attitude of giving up on action because the goal seems out of reach. Despair means realising that there is no God who can help us to get things that are beyond our control. For Sartre, we should not concern ourselves with such things (for example, getting angry because the train is not on time).

Determinism   The view that all events, including human action, are the necessary result of prior events. This means that whatever happens is necessarily caused by what precedes it, and that it could not have been any different. The successes of modern science in explaining the universe in a deterministic way has helped to give weight to determinism. Philosophers are not overly concerned about determinism in the natural world, but they do get agitated when the question arises of whether humans are determined. One worrying consequence of determinism being applied to us is that, if our actions are determined, and we cannot help doing them, then why should we accept responsibility for them, since there was nothing we could do about them? In contrast to human determinism is the view that humans have **free will**, and that we are in some important way free from the chain of causes and effects that determines the rest of the universe. Sartre rejects determinism outright, saying that it is another form of **bad faith**. Sartre firmly believes in human **freedom**.

Disgust   For Sartre, we feel disgust when we first step outside of our ordinary way of looking at the world and we come to appreciate the absurdity of **existence**. In his novel *Nausea*, Sartre describes the feelings of a man who begins to see himself as existing for the first time. What follows from this realisation is that he sees that everything, including himself, is arbitrary, the world has no reason, everything in it is superfluous. Our disgust is our gut reaction to the meaninglessness of the world.

Essence   The essential, or defining, characteristics of something make up its essence. For example, the essence of a square is to have four straight sides joining each other at 90°. Without these characteristics a shape would not be a square. Many philosophers argue that there are defining characteristics of a human being, in other words that humans have an essence. Sartre rejects this essentialism, arguing that we have no essence and that nothing defines us.

Ethics   See **morality**.

Existence   Sartre distinguishes between 'existence' and 'being', associating the former with **being-for-itself** and the latter with **being-in-itself**. To 'be' is a passive state, with no possibility of change, no **freedom**. It means having an **essence**. So, an object such as a paper-knife is just what it is: a knife used to cut open paper. To 'exist', on the other hand, is to be free, to be conscious of our freedom and to have the power to **transcend** our past and present circumstances. So, a waiter is not what he is: he can choose at any moment to reject his position as a waiter.

Existence precedes essence   Sartre claims that all existentialists hold in common the belief that for humans 'our **existence** comes before our **essence**'. There are difficulties analysing this idea, but it seems to mean either that humans exist and have no essence (until we die) or that humans exist but are free to create

and recreate temporary 'essences'. This is in contrast to objects, **being-in-itself**, whose essence or defining properties come before their existence.

Existentialism   A term coined in 1943 by Gabriel Marcel to describe the philosophy of Jean-Paul Sartre and Simone de Beauvoir. It gradually came to refer to any philosophical theory that places an emphasis on our individual awareness of **existence**. So, existentialist philosophies can be contrasted with other type of philosophies, such as rationalism or empiricism, which make claims that go beyond the individual's experience of the world and of existence. Sartre claimed that all existentialists believed that human **existence precedes essence**, although not everyone would agree that this is the best definition of existentialism. Existentialism eventually came to be associated with a way of life (café and jazz club culture), a type of fashion (black polo necks and trousers) and even music (Juliette Greco).

Facticity   Those facts, or things that are true of us, over which we have no control. Our facticity includes: our past, which we cannot change; our **freedom**, which we did not choose but is part of **being-for-itself**; our bodies; the laws of physics; our place of birth and upbringing. For Sartre, all of these things provide a context to our freedom, the concrete situation in which we find ourselves and within which or against which we act.

Freedom/free will   Freedom can refer to metaphysical freedom, or freedom of the will, or other social freedoms, such as freedom to vote or freedom from wrongful arrest. Sartre is concerned with both types of freedom, although his existentialist theory places most emphasis on our metaphysical freedom. For Sartre, our freedom is just an unavoidable fact about us, we are 'condemned to be free'. Freedom should not be confused with omnipotence; it does not mean being able to have whatever we wish. Our freedom exists within the context of our **facticity**.

Human nature   The essential qualities of all human beings. Since the time of Plato, western philosophers have held differing views on human nature but, for Sartre, all theories of human nature are mistaken because they suggest that we have an **essence**.

Humanism   Unlike many other 'isms', humanism is not a coherent philosophical movement, but is a term used to describe any theory which places human beings at the centre of things. Humanism has a distinctly moral slant because it also tends to place value on human beings, and to place the origin of value in human beings. Sartre was concerned by attacks on existentialism, which claimed that it was not a humanism, and gave the lecture *E & H* to defend existentialism and to show that it is a humanism after all.

Intentionality   A term used by the German **phenomenologist** Husserl to describe the 'object-directed' nature of consciousness. Our consciousness, or our awareness, is always 'of' something. In other words, it is always directed on to something.

Intersubjectivity   Intersubjectivity occurs where there is an agreement between two or more '**subjectivities**' or individual minds. Intersubjectivity may be the nearest thing that we can get to '**objectivity**', which is the position of knowing things as they really are. For Sartre, intersubjectivity means the interdependence of individual subjectivity: that my consciousness and my awareness of my freedom depend upon your recognising these things in me, and vice versa. Intersubjectivity lies at the heart of Sartre's existentialist morality.

Look, the   Sartre describes how we become immediately aware of other people (**being-for-itself**) through their look (in French *le Regard*). It makes us feel self-conscious or ashamed or embarrassed. Through the Look, other people try to fix us with an **essence**, whilst we, through our look, try to fix them with an essence. In *B & N*, Sartre uses this idea of the conflict of the Look to sum up the essential conflict that always exists between us and other people.

Mauvaise foi   See **bad faith**.

Metaphysical freedom   See **freedom**.

Metaphysics/metaphysical   The area of philosophy concerned with what the world is really and truly like. For example, the debate about **free will** versus **determinism** is a metaphysical debate, because it seeks to find out whether or not humans are ultimately free or determined.

Morality   In philosophical terms a moral theory is a theory that prescribes how we should or should not act and what we should or should not do with our lives. Some philosophers have argued that morality is **objective**, that it exists independently of human beings, whilst other philosophers have argued that morality is **subjective**, that it has its origins only in individual human beings. Sartre's moral philosophy may be characterised as subjective, because he thinks that each of us creates moral values in our actions.

Nihilism   The claim that **morality** cannot be justified, and so might as well be rejected. So, nihilists do not believe in any moral values and do whatever they want to do. Sartre was concerned that existentialism was getting a reputation as a nihilistic theory, one that encouraged 'moral anarchy', and his lecture, *E & H*, sets out partly to defend **existentialism** against such claims.

Nothingness   Sartre argued that the heart of **being-for-itself** is nothingness. We can try to understand this very difficult idea by thinking of it as a 'gap' or a 'hole' that exists between us and our past, or us and our future. Sartre does not think that we, as **self-conscious** beings, have an **essence**; nothing defines us. This means that we are free from our past, in a way that a chair or a dog is not. It also means that our future is full of possibilities, again in a way that it is not for a chair or a dog.

Objectify   To treat someone as an object. When we **look** at another person we give them an **essence**, we pigeon-hole them, even though we know that they do not have an essence but are free like us. In *B & N*, Sartre believed that we are doomed to objectify other people, but in *E & H* and his later works he put forward a much more optimistic view.

Objective/objectivity   An objective viewpoint or judgement is to be contrasted with a **subjective** one. Objectivity implies an impersonal or absolute perspective on things, and it is a goal to which most philosophers have aspired. However, **phenomenologists** and **existentialists** say that objectivity is impossible, and argue that we must begin philosophy from the subjective.

Other, the   Sartre talks about other people as 'the Other'. He puts forward a very negative account of our relationship with the Other in

B & N: it is doomed to conflict as we try to **objectify** each other through the **Look**. In *E & H*, Sartre begins to reveal the possibility of more optimistic relations with the Other as he argues that we must respect their freedom.

Paradox of freedom   Sartre claims on the one hand that we are absolutely free, but on the other hand that we are 'condemned to be free'. In other words, even though we are free, we cannot choose not to be free. This apparent contradiction can be resolved once we have in place the concept of **facticity**. Our freedom is just one of those facts about us that we cannot change, but that does not mean we are not free.

Phenomenology   A method of doing philosophy which carefully focuses on the individual's consciousness, and the objects of their consciousness. Through this process of rigorous introspection some phenomenologists, such as Husserl, argued that we would gradually come to know the **essence** of things. Sartre uses phenomenology in a different way: he relies on the insights of phenomenology to carefully describe the world as it is experienced by all human beings. For Sartre, all human experiences, physical, emotional, intellectual, are thus the proper subject of philosophy as they are all equally revealing and equally significant.

Quietism   An attitude of resignation to the world to the extent that we can no longer be bothered to act. Sartre connects quietism to **despair**, as we may give up on action when we realise that so much of the world is beyond our control, that there seems no point in doing anything. In particular, quietism may strike us when we realise that after we die all our good works may come to nothing: so why do anything?

Scum   In *E & H*, Sartre identifies scum as those people who are in **bad faith** because they think their existence is necessary. They are mistaken. Elsewhere in Sartre's fiction he condemns the scum for going on to conclude that they are somehow more valuable than other people, and for seeking to impose their values on other people.

Self-consciousness   Consciousness is **intentional**, in other words it is always aimed at or directed upon something else. Self-consciousness arises when consciousness turns its attention inwards on to itself.

Self-deception   See **bad faith**.

Self-surpassing   Our ability to go beyond (transcend or surpass) our past and present selves is a key feature of **freedom**. Because we are **being-for-itself** we have no **essence** and so we are able to reinvent ourselves throughout our lives.

Spirit of seriousness   In *B & N*, Sartre talks about the 'serious man' or the 'spirit of seriousness' when he is referring to people who believe in any form of objective **morality**. Such people believe that values are 'out there' waiting to be discovered, and place humans below these values. However, according to Sartre, this is a form of **bad faith**, as it is a denial of the fact that we invent all values through our actions.

Subjective/subjectivity   A subjective judgement or viewpoint is in contrast to an **objective** one. It is a perspective drawn from a single individual (a subject). Some philosophers, such as Kierkegaard, have argued that a subjective approach is the only possible approach to philosophy. Sartre argued that we must begin philosophy with subjectivity, in other words start with the individual subject's experiences and consciousness.

Supernal artisan   Supernal means 'divine' or 'heavenly' and artisan means 'crafts person'. This is the phrase Sartre uses to refer to God, who was supposed to have designed the world.

Transcendent   See **self-surpassing**.

Universalisability   Something is universalisable if we can make it universal without falling into inconsistency. Kant believed that an action was moral if the rule underpinning it was universalisable, in other words, if the rule could be made universal without inconsistency. Sartre seems to hold a similar position in *E & H* when he asks us to pose the question 'what would happen if everyone did as I am doing?'

Notes

Chapter 2

1 Jean-Paul Sartre, *Words* (trans. Irene Clephane), Penguin, 1979, p. 14.

2 'Conversations with Sartre', in Simone de Beauvoir, *Adieux: A Farewell to Sartre*, Penguin, 1988, p. 296.

3 Sartre openly confessed to writing his most incomprehensible book, *Critique of Dialectical Reason*, under the influence of drugs. In an atypical understatement Sartre goes on to say of his *Critique* that 'it is not a masterpiece of planning, composition and clarity' ('Conversations with Sartre', in Simone de Beauvoir, *Adieux: A Farewell to Sartre*, Penguin, 1988, pp. 174, 318).

4 Following this experiment Sartre said, 'I am on the edge of hallucinatory psychosis' (Simone de Beauvoir, *The Prime of Life*, Penguin, 1965, p. 210).

5 For three alternative accounts of Sartre's escape from prison camp, see Geoffrey Wall, 'Portrait of Sartre', in Sartre, *Modern Times: Selected Non-Fiction*, Penguin, 2000, p. xxvii.

6 For a brief account of this period of resistance, see Kenneth Thompson, *Sartre: Life and Works*, Facts on File, 1984, pp. 46–7.

7 Simone de Beauvoir, *Force of Circumstance*, André Deutsch, 1965, p. 48.

8 Sartre said that he liked the constant bustle and indifferent attitude of café life: no one would bother him or worry about whether they were disturbing him (Michel Contat and Michel Rybalka, *The Writings of Jean-Paul Sartre*, Northwestern University Press, 1974, p. 149).

9 He refused it because he did not wish to be aligned with any political institution, and did not wish to compromise his position as a writer and critic (Jean-Paul Sartre, 'The writer should refuse to let himself be turned into an institution', in *Le Monde*, October 1964).

10 Simone de Beauvoir, *Adieux: A Farewell to Sartre*, Penguin, 1988, p. 423.

11 Simone de Beauvoir, *Adieux: A Farewell to Sartre*, Penguin, 1988, p. 127.

12 'Philosophers have only interpreted the world, in various ways; the point is to change it.' Karl Marx and Friedrich Engels, 'Theses on Feuerbach' Section XI (in CJ Arthur [ed.], *The German Ideology: A Student's Edition*, Lawrence and Wishart, 1970).

13 For a description of the explosion in 'existentialist' café and club culture in 1940s Paris, see Claude Francis and Fernande Gontier, *Simone de Beauvoir: A Life; A Love Story*, St Martin's Press, 1987, p. 218 ff. For Hollywood's version of the existentialists, see *Funny Face* (directed by Stanley Donen, 1956) and *An American in Paris* (directed by Vincente Minnelli, 1951).

14 For a more detailed account of the lecture, see Annie Cohen-Solal, *Sartre: A Life*, Gallimard, 1985, p. 247 ff.

15 For example, Jean Kanapa, a communist and ex-friend of Simone de Beauvoir, wrote an article entitled 'Existentialism is not a Humanism', in *Les Editions Sociales*, 1946.

16 Sartre once said of his work that he wanted 'to make a philosophy of man in a material world' (Simone de Beauvoir, *Adieux: A Farewell to Sartre*, Penguin, 1988, p. 436).

17 Mary Warnock, *The Philosophy of Sartre*, Hutchinson, 1966, p. 72.

18 One of his most notorious examples is his description of a human 'as a being which is what it is not and which is not what it is' (*Being and Nothingness*, Methuen, 1977, p. 58). We shall try to unpick this paradoxical statement later, in note 37.

19 Towards the end of his life, in conversation with de Beauvoir, Sartre gave a frank account of his attitudes to and relationships with women (Simone de Beauvoir, *Adieux: A Farewell to Sartre*, Penguin, 1988 p. 290 ff).

Chapter 4

20 Apparently Sartre turned 'pale with emotion' at this new approach to philosophy (Simone de Beauvoir, *The Prime of Life* (trans. P. Green), Penguin, 1965, p. 135).

21 Mary Warnock, *The Philosophy of Sartre*, Hutchinson, 1966, p. 73.

22 René Descartes, *Discourse on Method*, Part IV (in *Descartes, Selected Philosophical Writings*, Cambridge University Press, 1993).

23 Franz Brentano, *Psychology from an Empirical Standpoint* (trans. A. Rancurello, D.B. Terrell and L. McAlaister), Humanities Press, 1973; see, for example, p. 88.

24 It was Gabriel Marcel who first applied the term 'existentialism' to Sartre's philosophy in 1943. Sartre's famous response, at a conference in Belgium in 1945, was to say: 'My philosophy is a philosophy of Existence; I don't even know what existentialism is' (quoted in Simone de Beauvoir, *Force of Circumstance*, André Deutsch, 1965, p. 38). Clearly, by the end of that year, Sartre was comfortable with using that term in reference to his own philosophy.

25 Marcel Proust wrote several volumes of his masterpiece, *A la Recherche du Temps Perdu* (trans. as *In Search Of Lost Time*), Penguin, 2002.

26 Stephen Priest (ed.), *Jean-Paul Sartre: Basic Writings*, Routledge, 2001, p. 25.

27 Jean-Paul Sartre, *Huis Clos and Other Plays*, Penguin, 2000.

28 For a different solution to this problem, see Stephen Priest (ed.), *Jean-Paul Sartre: Basic Writings*, Routledge, 2001, pp. 24–5. Priest suggests that Sartre in *E & H* is dividing the world into three types of things: humans, artefacts and naturally occurring objects. On this interpretation the idea of 'design' applies only to artefacts, and not to naturally occurring objects, hence there is no implication of design in the natural world.

29 For further discussion of this interpretation of Sartre, see Gregory McCulloch, *Using Sartre*, Routledge, 2001, p. 59.

30 Fyodor Dostoyevsky, *The Brothers Karamazov*, Bantam, 1981, p. 80. Sartre's 'quotation' from Dostoyevsky (on p. 33 of *E & H*) is a conflation of the quotation on page 80 with another from later in the book: 'How can there be crime, if God does not exist?' (*The Brothers Karamazov*, p. 381).

31 Although Sartre does offer 'proofs' of God's non-existence in *B & N*, the most significant argument revolves around the claim that God's essence is His existence, which Sartre says is an impossibility (see David Cooper *Existentialism*, Blackwell, 2000, p. 146 ff, for a very clear breakdown of Sartre's arguments in *B & N*). Later on in life Sartre said, 'In *Being and Nothingness* I set out reasons for my denial of God's existence that were not

actually the real reasons. The real reasons were much more direct and childish.' The 'real reason' to which Sartre is referring here is the revelation he had when he was twelve that God did not exist (Simone de Beauvoir, *Adieux: A Farewell to Sartre*, Penguin, 1988 p. 438).

32 However, David Cooper points out that the examples Sartre gives on page 26 of *E & H* are problematic: Jaspers is not a Christian in the traditional sense of the word, nor is Heidegger a clear-cut atheist (David Cooper, *Existentialism*, Blackwell, 2000, p. 146).

33 Jean-Paul Sartre, *Being and Nothingness*, Methuen, 1977, p. 10.

34 Jean-Paul Sartre, *Words*, Penguin, 1979, p. 58.

35 Jean-Paul Sartre, *Being and Nothingness*, Methuen, 1977, p. 33.

36 Jean-Paul Sartre, *Being and Nothingness*, Methuen, 1977, p. 30.

37 We saw earlier (note 18) that Sartre describes humans 'as a being [1] which is what it is not and [2] which is not what it is' (*Being and Nothingness*, Methuen, 1977, p. 58). We are now in a position to try to unravel this paradoxical assertion:
   [1] Humans are nothingness, and our future, which has not yet happened, is up to us to choose ('we are what we are not').
   [2] Humans do not have an essence, and so anything that we are at the moment or have done in the past (for example, being a student) does not define us for the rest of our life ('we are not what we are').

■ Chapter 5

38 David Cooper makes the point that some philosophers do make the mistake, when discussing existentialist freedom, of talking about it as if it were a value to be 'preserved and increased' (David Cooper, *Existentialism*, Blackwell, 2000, p. 154).

39 Jean-Paul Sartre, *Being and Nothingness*, Methuen, 1977, p. 483.

40 During the Nazi occupation of France, in 1944, Sartre wrote an article beginning with the words, 'We have never been more free than under the German Occupation' ('The Republic of Silence', printed in the journal *Les Lettres Françaises*, September 1944). No matter the physical or political limits imposed upon us, we are still free to choose our attitude and our response to these obstacles.

41 Simone de Beauvoir, *The Second Sex*, Penguin, 1987. See, for example, p. 295.

42 This is a position developed by Gregory McCulloch in *Using Sartre*, Routledge, 2001, p. 38 ff.

43 Jean-Paul Sartre, *Being and Nothingness*, Methuen, 1977, p. 40.

44 Jean-Paul Sartre, *Being and Nothingness*, Methuen, 1977, p. 553.

45 Jean-Paul Sartre, *Being and Nothingness*, Methuen, 1977, p. 41.

46 For more on freedom and live possibilities, read Gregory McCulloch, *Using Sartre*, Routledge, 2001, pp. 38–50, 64–70. However, McCulloch, despite his argument, seems worried by the possibility of giving up his career as a professional philosopher.

47 Sartre writes, 'I choose myself perpetually . . . my freedom eats away at my freedom' (*Being and Nothingness*, Methuen, 1977, p. 480).

48 As Sartre says, in *B & N*, ' "to be free" does not mean "to obtain what one has wished" but by oneself "to determine oneself to wish". ' In other words, being free is not about getting whatever we want, in the way that an omnipotent being could, but about deciding what we do want and striving for it. 'Success is not important to freedom' (*Being and Nothingness*, Methuen, 1977, p. 483).

49 He says similar things ('I am condemned to be free') in *Being and Nothingness* (Methuen, 1977); see, for example, p. 439 or 485.

50 Sartre identifies the most important features of our facticity as: 'my place, my body, my past, my environment, my fellow humans, and my death' (*Being and Nothingness*, Methuen, 1977, pp. 489–553).

51 Sartre gives a detailed example of someone who is hiking and who, after a few hours, begins to feel tired and gives up. Sartre's point is that the tiredness did not cause the hiker to give up, he *chose* to stop walking. Giving up was his response to this particular obstacle. He could have chosen to have carried on walking, to have been spurred on by his fatigue, rather than crushed by it (*Being and Nothingness*, Methuen, 1977, pp. 453–6).

52 De Beauvoir disagreed with Sartre on this point, arguing that there was in fact a 'heirarchy of situations' from which people were more or less free to escape (Claude Francis and Fernande Gontier, *Simone de Beauvoir: A Life; A Love Story*, St Martin's Press, 1987, pp. 210–11).

53 Sartre gives a very philosophical account of his attempt to stop smoking (*Being and Nothingness*, Methuen, 1977, pp. 596–7).

54 Maurice Merleau-Ponty, *The Phenomenology of Perception*, Routledge, 1962, p. 437 ff.

55 Towards the end of his life, Sartre reread a preface he had written to a collection of wartime plays. He commented, 'I had written "Whatever the circumstances . . . a man is always free to choose to be a traitor or not" . . . It's incredible, I actually believed that' (*New York Review of Books*, March 1970, p. 22).

Chapter 6

56 Gregory McCulloch argues that we can answer this question by distinguishing between 'feeling anguish' and 'being subject to anguish'. We are subject to anguish all the time, but it is only when we start to reflect on our behaviour (for example, our daily routine) that we start to feel anguish (Gregory McCulloch, *Using Sartre*, Routledge, 2001, p. 47).

57 Sartre writes, 'I am *abandoned* in the world . . . I find myself suddenly alone and without help' (*Being and Nothingness*, Methuen, 1977, pp. 555–6). This is another fact about us that we can do nothing to change; abandonment is thus part of our facticity for Sartre.

58 Sartre describes his own revelation at the age of twelve: 'One day I was walking up and down outside [my friends'] house waiting for them to get ready. I don't know where the thought came from or how it struck me, yet all at once I said to myself, "But God doesn't exist!" ' (Simone de Beauvoir, *Adieux: A Farewell to Sartre*, Penguin, 1988, p. 434).

59 The Scottish philosopher, David Hume, argued that action was either uncaused (and hence random) or caused (by our inner mental state). He rejected the first in favour of the second, but still maintained that such an 'internally caused' action was a free one: a position that came to be known as compatibilism (David Hume, *An Enquiry Concerning Human Understanding*, Section 90).

60 For an excellent account of the psychology of moral decision-making found in Sartre, read David Jopling's essay, 'Sartre's moral psychology', in Christina Howells (ed.), *The Cambridge Companion to Sartre*, Cambridge University Press, 1999.

61 David Cooper attempts to give a coherent account of Sartre's position in Cooper, *Existentialism*, Blackwell, 2000, p. 157 ff.

Chapter 7

62 Jean-Paul Sartre, *Being and Nothingness*, Methuen, 1977, p. 626.

63 Simone de Beauvoir, *The Ethics of Ambiguity* (trans. Bernard Frechtman), Citadel Press, 1948.

64 Mary Warnock, *Existentialist Ethics*, Macmillan, 1967, p. 2.

65 Jean-Paul Sartre, *Being and Nothingness*, Methuen, 1977, pp. 47–70.

66 Jean-Paul Sartre, *Being and Nothingness*, Methuen, 1977, p. 566. Sartre says that the idea that a being for-itself (which is free and has no essence) could become in-itself (which has no essence) is a contradictory idea. Yet he also says that deep down humans have a passionate desire to obtain an essence, something which is impossible. In this sense, then, he concludes, 'Man is a useless passion' (*B & N*, p. 615).

67 For a whole series of examples of characters in bad faith drawn from Sartre's fiction, see Brian Masters, *A Student's Guide to Jean-Paul Sartre*, Heinemann, 1989, p. 22 ff.

68 Jean-Paul Sartre, *Being and Nothingness*, Methuen, 1977, pp. 55–6. In one of his short stories, Sartre describes a woman who is trying to leave her husband, with the help of her friend. She lets herself be pushed and pulled like a doll, as her husband yanks her back whilst her friend tugs her to freedom ('Intimacy', in *The Wall and other stories*, New Directions, 1969).

69 Brian Masters finds lots of examples in Sartre's fiction of scum who also seek to impose their value system on others. According to Masters, the scum put themselves above others and oppress and rob freedom from others who are not like them (*A Student's Guide to Jean-Paul Sartre*, Heinemann, 1989, pp. 31–4).

70 *On The Waterfront*, directed by Elia Kazan, 1954.

71 This was a belief which Sartre held long after he had given up existentialism as a doctrine. At the end of his life, Sartre reflected on what he had done and said: 'So when I die I shall not die as many people do, saying "Oh, if I had my life to live over again I should live it in another way" . . . No, I accept myself entirely and feel that I am exactly what I wanted to be' (Simone de Beauvoir, *Adieux: A Farewell to Sartre*, Penguin, 1988, p. 433).

72 Mary Warnock, *Existentialist Ethics*, Macmillan, 1967, p. 33.

73 Simone de Beauvoir goes further in her condemnation of those in bad faith, referring to such people as 'sub-men' (Simone de Beauvoir, *The Ethics of Ambiguity*, trans. Bernard Frechtman, Citadel Press, 1948, p. 42 ff).

74 See, for example, *E & H*, p. 33; or *Being & Nothingness* Methuen, 1977, p. 626.

75 Gregory McCulloch argues that bad faith does not necessarily imply self-deception. He suggests that it is more coherent to interpret Sartre's concept of bad faith as a type of conceptual muddle or error that we fall into, and not as a deliberate act of self-deception (Gregory McCulloch, *Using Sartre*, Routledge 2001, pp. 62–4).

76 George Orwell, *1984*, Penguin, 1982, p. 172.

77 Jean-Paul Sartre, *Being and Nothingness*, Methuen, 1977, p. 51 ff.

78 Both Gregory McCulloch (*Using Sartre*, Routledge, 2001, p. 61) and David Cooper (*Existentialism*, Blackwell, 2000, p. 119) think of bad faith in terms of our failure to 'get the balance right' in this way.

79 Jean-Paul Sartre, *Being and Nothingness*, Methuen, 1977, p. 50.

80 In a footnote on p. 70 of *Being and Nothingness* (Methuen, 1977), Sartre suggests that we can 'radically escape' from acting in bad faith via an act of self-recovery which he calls authenticity, but he says that a description of authenticity has no place in that book. In the final four pages of *B & N* (entitled 'Ethical implications'), Sartre discusses how we can become conscious of our freedom and can begin to see it as the source of all values. This is the springboard for his discussion of an authentic existence in *E & H*.

81 Both Sartre and de Beauvoir were shocked by witnessing a young female friend of theirs pushing a lit cigarette into the back of her hand (Simone de Beauvoir, *The Prime of Life*, Penguin, 1965, p. 258). In Sartre's fiction his characters often behave in a gratuitous way when confronted with their freedom, for example, by inserting a knife into their palms (Jean-Paul Sartre, *The Age of Reason*, Penguin, 1981, pp. 194–5).

82 Jean-Paul Sartre, *Being and Nothingness*, Methuen, 1977, p. 364.

83 See, for example, *E & H*, pp. 51–2.

84 Jean-Paul Sartre, *Being and Nothingness*, Methuen, 1977, pp. 254–61.

85 The character who says this is Garcin: 'You remember all we were told about the torture-chambers, the fire, the brimstone . . . Old wives' tales! There's no need for red-hot pokers. Hell is . . . other people' (Jean-Paul Sartre, *Huis Clos and Other Plays*, Penguin, 2000, p. 223).

86 Sartre said that the famous phrase 'Hell is other people', from his play *No Exit*, had always been misinterpreted. He meant by this that if our relationships with other people are bad, then we come to live in hell with them. Sartre said that this is because we depend on other people for our judgement of ourselves, and so, if the 'mirror' of the other person is twisted, if they hate us, then hatred informs the way we see ourselves (quoted in Michel Contat and Michel Rybalka, *The Writings of Jean-Paul Sartre*, Northwestern University Press, 1974, p. 99).

87 Thomas Anderson gives a very good account of the interdependence of subjectivity in *Sartre's Two Ethics*, Open Court, 1993, Chapter 5.

88 For a powerful and impassioned attack on European colonialism, which robbed much of the world of its political freedom, read Sartre's preface to Frantz Fanon's *Wretched of the Earth*, Penguin, 1967, pp. 1–26.

■ Chapter 8

89 John Stuart Mill, *Utilitarianism*, Fontana, 1985; Aristotle, *Ethics*, Penguin, 1976.

90 For example, see Jean-Paul Sartre, *Being and Nothingness*, Methuen, 1977, pp. 39–40, 580, 626; and *E & H*, p. 51.

91 Almost thirty years after *E & H*, de Beauvoir (mis)quoted Dostoyevsky (see note 30) back to Sartre: ' "If God does not exist, everything is permitted." You don't believe that, do you?' To which Sartre replied: 'In one way I clearly see what [Dostoyevsky] means, and abstractly it's true; but in another way I clearly see that killing a man is wrong. It is directly, absolutely wrong' (Simone de Beauvoir, *Adieux: A Farewell To Sartre*, Penguin, 1988, p. 439). We can see *E & H* as one of Sartre's first public attempts to square his belief that morality is invented by humans, with his belief that we must all respect certain values, such as the freedom of other people.

92 Kant's original idea of a universal law can be found in his 'Ground Work of the Metaphysic of Morals' in *The Moral Law* (trans. H.J. Paton), Hutchinson, 1972, p. 83.

93 Immanuel Kant, *The Moral Law*, Hutchinson, 1972, p. 101.

94 In the twentieth century there were some philosophers, such as Richard Hare (*The Language of Morals*, Oxford University Press, 1952), who advocated the view that the meaning of moral language is that it is prescriptive, in other words, it tells other people what to do.

95 David Cooper refers to this as 'reciprocal freedom', referring to the entwinement of each of our individual freedoms with everyone else's (*Existentialism*, Blackwell, 2000, p. 187).

96 Simone de Beauvoir echoes this argument in *The Ethics of Ambiguity*. However, she does not think that we should unconditionally value the other's freedom: 'We have to respect freedom only when it is intended for freedom . . . A freedom which is interested only in denying freedom must be denied.' In other words, if we use our freedom to oppress and imprison someone, then that person does not need to respect our freedom (*The Ethics of Ambiguity*, trans. Bernard Frechtman, Citadel Press, 1948, pp. 90–1).

97 De Beauvoir also locates existential morality in authenticity. For her, 'Ethics is the triumph of freedom over facticity.' So, we must embrace our freedom and use it to transcend our past and our present circumstances (Simone de Beauvoir, *The Ethics of Ambiguity*, trans. Bernard Frechtman, Citadel Press, 1948, p. 42).

98 Jean-Paul Sartre, *Notebooks for an Ethics*, University of Chicago Press, 1992, p. 499 ff. Here Sartre consciously rejects the position he had put forward in *B & N*, that the other is always a threat to our freedom.

99 Mary Warnock mentions this idea in her *Existentialist Ethics*, Macmillan, 1967, pp. 40–1.

100 Jean-Paul Sartre, *Being and Nothingness*, Methuen, 1977, p. 412. (See also p. 73 of this book.) Sartre also says that '*Being and Nothingness* is an ontology before conversion' (*Notebooks for an Ethics*, University of Chicago Press, 1992, p. 4).

101 For example, Linda A. Bell, *Sartre's Ethics of Authenticity*, University of Alabama Press, 1989; Simone de Beauvoir, *Force of Circumstance*, André Deutsch, 1965, p. 5.

■ Chapter 9

102 Simone de Beauvoir referred to these times as 'the Existentialist Offensive' (*Force of Circumstance*, André Deutsch, 1965, p. 38).

103 In France this was an act of rebellion akin to rejecting a knighthood in the United Kingdom. Sartre offered the same grounds for rejecting the Nobel Prize for Literature in 1964: he wished to remain free of all institutions so that he would never have to compromise his writing.

104 Jean-Paul Sartre, 'The nationalisation of literature', *Les Tempes Modernes*, 1945.

105 Most notably amongst communists and Catholics, both powerful lobbies in post-war France.

106 Critics were shocked that Sartre had placed the story of an abortion at the centre of the novel *The Age of Reason* (the first part of his 'Roads to Freedom' trilogy), published earlier in 1945. Sartre may also have been referring to critics' charges of obscenity, which were made against him following the publication in 1939 of his collection of short stories, *The Wall*.

107 At the end of 1944, Sartre published an article in the communist newspaper *Action*, entitled 'A more precise characterisation of existentialism'. The article was Sartre's response to two criticisms by communists, the first claiming that he was a follower of Heidegger (the German philosopher admired by the Nazis) and the second that existentialism is a distraction from the collective class struggle against the bourgeoisie. It is true that Sartre did draw on some of Heidegger's concepts when writing *B & N*, but there was no love lost between the two thinkers and in no sense was Sartre a disciple of Heidegger.

108 As de Beauvoir said, 'at the time Existentialism was being treated as a nihilist philosophy, wilfully pessimistic, frivolous, licentious, despairing and ignoble; some defence had to be made' (Simone de Beauvoir, *Force of Circumstance*, André Deutsch, 1965, p. 67). However, she thought that her own attempt at a defence, *The Ethics of Ambiguity*, wasted time rebutting some of the more absurd criticisms.

109 This process would take longer than a few weeks. A month after the lecture, a journalist came to interview Sartre, and this is how Simone de Beauvoir describes the article that the journalist eventually wrote: 'Sartre found a garbage can had been emptied over him: sordid and frivolous, his philosophy was fit for people who were sick, morally and physically; his sole delight was filth' (Simone de Beauvoir, *Force of Circumstance*, André Deutsch, 1965, p 43).

110 It is unfortunate that one of the best-known stories in existentialist fiction, Albert Camus' *The Outsider*, revolves around an apparently under-motivated murder by the protagonist, Meursault. For Sartre, this would not be the act of an existentialist hero.

111 Jean-Paul Sartre, *Nausea*, Penguin, 1965, pp. 175–6.

112 Jean Cocteau was a French writer, poet, artist and film-maker.

113 Years later, Sartre revived his attack on this kind of inauthentic humanism. He said of European humanism that it placed Europeans above everyone and gave them an excuse to enslave other nations: 'It was nothing but an ideology of lies, a perfect justification to pillage; its honeyed words, its affectation of sensibility were only alibis for our aggressions' (Jean-Paul Sartre, 'Preface', in Frantz Fanon, *Wretched of the Earth*, Penguin, 1967, p. 21).

Selected bibliography

Essential reading

Sartre, Jean-Paul, *Existentialism and Humanism* (trans. Philip Mairet), Methuen, 1973

Recommended reading

Cooper, David, *Existentialism*, Blackwell, 2000

Hayman, Ronald, *Sartre: A Biography*, Carroll & Graf, 1992

McCulloch, Gregory, *Using Sartre*, Routledge, 2001

Myerson, George, *Sartre's Existentialism and Humanism – A Beginner's Guide*, Hodder & Stoughton, 2002

Priest, Stephen, *Jean-Paul Sartre: Basic Writings*, Routledge, 2001

Sartre, Jean-Paul, *Essays in Existentialism*, Citadel Press, 1993

Sartre, Jean-Paul, *Huis Clos and Other Plays*, Penguin, 2000

Sartre, Jean-Paul, *Nausea*, Penguin, 1965

Sartre, Jean-Paul, *The Wall and other stories*, New Directions, 1969

Sartre, Jean-Paul, *Words*, Penguin, 2000

Thompson, Kenneth A., *Sartre: Life and Works*, Facts on File, 1984

Warbuton, Nigel, 'A student's guide to Jean-Paul Sartre's *Existentialism and Humanism*' *Philosophy Now*, issue 15, spring/summer 1996

Warnock, Mary, *Existentialist Ethics*, Macmillan, 1967

Warnock, Mary, *The Philosophy of Sartre*, Hutchinson, 1966

Further reading

Anderson, Thomas C., *Sartre's Two Ethics*, Open Court, 1993

Baldwin, Thomas, 'Sartre, Existentialism and Humanism', in G. Vesey (ed.), *Philosophers, Ancient and Modern*, Cambridge University Press, 1985

Catalano, Joseph, *A Commentary on Jean-Paul Sartre's 'Being and Nothingness'*, University of Chicago Press, 1980

De Beauvoir, Simone, *Adieux: A Farewell to Sartre* (trans. Patrick O'Brian), Penguin, 1988

De Beauvoir, Simone, *Force of Circumstance* (trans. Richard Howard), André Deutsch, 1965

De Beauvoir, Simone, *The Prime of Life* (trans. Peter Green), Penguin, 2001

De Beauvoir, Simone, *The Second Sex* (trans. H. M. Parshley), Penguin, 1987

Cohen-Solal, Annie, *Sartre: A Life*, Gallimard, 1985

Danto, Arthur C., *Sartre*, Fontana, 1985

Howells, Christina (ed.), *The Cambridge Companion to Sartre*, Cambridge University Press, 1999

Lloyd, Genevieve, *The Man of Reason*, Chapter 6, Methuen, 1984

Macquarrie, John, *Existentialism*, Penguin, 1991

Masters, Brian, *A Student's Guide to Jean-Paul Sartre*, Heinmann, 1989

Murdoch, Iris, *Sartre: Romantic Rationalist*, Chatto & Windus, 1987

Sartre, Jean-Paul, *Being and Nothingness* (trans. Hazel Barnes), Methuen, 1977

Sartre, Jean-Paul, *Notebooks for an Ethics*, University of Chicago Press, 1992

Warnock, Mary, *Ethics since 1900*, Oxford University Press, 1979

Warnock, Mary, *Existentialism*, Oxford University Press, 1970

Index